Management Ethics

Foundations of Business Ethics
Series editors: W. Michael Hoffman and Robert. E. Frederick

Written by an assembly of the most distinguished figures in business ethics, the Foundations of Business Ethics series aims to explain and assess the fundamental issues that motivate interest in each of the main subjects of contemporary research. In addition to a general introduction to business ethics, individual volumes cover key ethical issues in management, marketing, finance, accounting, and computing. The volumes, which are complementary yet complete in themselves, allow instructors maximum flexibility in the design and presentation of course materials without sacrificing either depth of coverage or the discipline-based focus of many business courses. The volumes can be used separately or in combination with anthologies and case studies, depending on the needs and interests of the instructors and students.

Management Ethics

Norman E. Bowie

with

Patricia H. Werhane

Blackwell
Publishing

BLACKWELL PUBLISHING
350 Main Street, Malden, MA 02148-5020, USA
108 Cowley Road, Oxford OX4 1JF, UK
550 Swanston Street, Carlton, Victoria 3053, Australia

First published 2005 by Blackwell Publishing Ltd

Library of Congress Cataloging-in-Publication Data

Bowie, Norman E., 1942–
Management ethics / Norman E. Bowie with Patricia H. Werhane
p. cm. — (Foundations of business ethics ; 5)
Includes bibliographical references and index.
ISBN 0-631-21472-0 (hardcover : alk. paper) — ISBN 0-631-21473-9 (pbk. :
alk. paper) 1. Business ethics. 2. Management—Moral and ethical aspects. 3.
Executives—Professional ethics. 4. Corporate governance—Moral and ethical
aspects. 5. Business logistics—Moral and ethical aspects. 6. Social
responsibility of business. I. Werhane, Patricia Hogue. II. Title. III. Series.

HF5387.B684 2004
174'.4—dc22
2004001786

A catalogue record for this title is available from the British Library.

Set in 10.5/12.5 Plantin
by MHL Production Services Ltd, Coventry, West Midlands
Printed and bound in the United Kingdom
by MPG Books Ltd, Bodmin, Cornwall

The publisher's policy is to use permanent paper from mills that operate a
sustainable forestry policy, and which has been manufactured from pulp
processed using acid-free and elementary chlorine-free practices.
Furthermore, the publisher ensures that the text paper and cover board used
have met acceptable environmental accreditation standards.

For further information on
Blackwell Publishing, visit our website:
http://www.blackwellpublishing.com

Contents

Preface

A book on management ethics is truly challenging for a number of reasons. And it is not for the reasons some might expect. You might expect that, given the current state of management ethics, it would be a short book. But that is not the case. There is too much to write about rather than too little. A manager will need to deal with almost every issue in business ethics, thus a book about management ethics is almost necessarily a book about business ethics in general. But that surely will not do since this book is one in a series of books on business ethics. Thus it must be a book about management ethics rather than a generic book on business ethics.

Our approach for avoiding this dilemma is to begin with the debate as to the proper role of the manager. Thus in chapter 1 we will be concerned about the duties that go with being a manager. In the next chapter we will ask: For whom is the manager an agent? The book takes a stakeholder approach. We will ask specifically what are the obligations of managers to employees (chapter 3), customers (chapter 4), non-traditional stakeholders (chapter 5), and the community (chapter 6). One inevitable question that arises in this stakeholder approach is: How far does the range of her obligations extend?

The remainder of the book will consider how we get managers to honor their obligations. Chapter 7 discusses the role of moral imagination in that regard and chapter 8 looks for the characteristics of the ethical leader. In the course of the book we will try to identify some of the features of business ethics that are unique to management ethics, such as executive compensation and supply chain management. Of course, even by limiting the discussion in this way, there will still be some unavoidable overlap with other topics in business ethics – the manager's obligation to the environment, for example. However, even in these overlap situations we will try to focus on the perspective of the manager.

We are deeply indebted to the series editor Robert Frederick, who has made many helpful suggestions about the manuscript. Several less than adequate arguments have been removed as a result of his careful reading. At several points he has had positive arguments of his own which we have incorporated into the text.

My Station and Its Duties: The Function of Being a Manager

Whenever someone asks, "What are my ethical obligations and responsibilities?" an answer to that question will necessarily be a function of the positions or roles one has in society. There are obligations that go with being a parent and there are also obligations that go with being a son or daughter. There are obligations unique to the role of teacher and also that of student. But given the time that one spends at work, perhaps the largest collection of obligations and responsibilities surrounds the occupation one has. There are obligations unique to being a doctor and obligations unique to being a lawyer. Given the role of manager, what are the obligations and responsibilities that accompany that role?

Certainly the place to begin a discussion of management ethics is with a description of the role of the manager. Once one knows the role, one will have some idea of the ethical obligations and responsibilities of a manger. But why will knowing the role determine the ethical obligations?

There are several answers to that question. One that appeals to many philosophers is based on an ethical theory that goes back to Plato and Aristotle. They believed that once you knew the function of something or the purpose of something, then you knew what the good was for that particular thing. To ask, "What is a good x?" is to ask, "What is the purpose of an x?" Once you knew what something was supposed to do or supposed to be, then you knew what a good one was. The purpose of medicine is to return people to health, so a good doctor is one who succeeds in returning people to health. The purpose of a military is to protect the state from its enemies and thus a good military is one that does that. So once we learn the purpose of management, we will know what a good manager is supposed to do. In other words, we will know what the obligations and responsibilities of a manager are.

However, that may seem like a strange way of putting the question. The manager is not independent like the doctor; the manager works for another. The key to management ethics is to determine whom the manager manages for. For whom is he or she an agent? And the answer to that question is one of the most controversial in management ethics.

This issue becomes crucial because of the reality that Berle and Means discussed in the 1930s – the separation of ownership and control.[1] The owners of the publicly-held corporation are the stockholders but there is no easy way to monitor the managers who are hired to manage the corporation on their behalf. The stockholders are not at the factory; indeed the vast majority of stockholders will never be at the factory. Thus we have the ultimate question: Who will manage the manager?

If you believe that people will always or even usually seek to benefit themselves at the expense of others whenever their interests conflict, then the question of who will manage the manager becomes a very important one. Finance theorists refer to this as an agency problem. Much that has been written about corporate governance attempts to address this problem. Good governance exercised by the board of directors is supposed to bring the actions of the chief executive officer (CEO) and other corporate officials (managers) into line with the interests of the stockholders. We will explore some of the mechanisms that are put into place to make sure that managers manage for the owners, but such mechanisms still do not solve our problem. If the board of directors is supposed to manage the CEO and the other top executives in the company, who is supposed to manage the board?

Now one could be an optimist about human nature. One could believe that human beings in responsible positions are motivated by the relatively high level of compensation and the attitude of being a professional so that they will work diligently for the owners without having to be extensively monitored. True professionals do not need to be monitored, one could argue.

Alas, the evidence, including much recent evidence, is not encouraging. A series of accounting and reporting scandals at the end of 2001 that continued through late 2003 have shaken the American capitalist system. Questions about the quality of a company's balance sheet and charges of financial irregularities and accounting misrepresentation were raised about many of the best companies in America. The epitome of the scandal was the Enron Corporation and its auditor Arthur Andersen. In some cases the board of directors and especially the audit committee of the board failed to exercise due diligence. They pretty much accepted whatever the management team said. In some cases the board or some member of the board worked in conjunction with members of the management team on these questionable practices. It is no wonder that questions about the duties of managers and how to solve the agency problem are at the top of the agenda.

Our analysis is complicated by a couple of factors that would distinguish the role obligations of doctors from the role obligations of managers.[2] At least until recently there has been no ambiguity about the function of the doctor and who the client is. The client is the patient and the function of the doctor is to treat illness and bring about health to the extent that it is scientifically possible.[3] However, as we shall see, there are two powerful competing theories regarding whom the manager serves as an agent. One view argues that primacy is to be given to the stockholder and that the manager is the agent of the stockholder. The competing view argues that various stakeholders of the firm have sufficient claims on the public corporation that the manager stands in an agency relationship to them. Those who take the stockholder approach think that the function of management is to focus on profits to the stockholders. Those who take the broader stakeholder approach think that the function of managers is to balance the interests of the various stakeholders so that a concern with profits is only one basic function of management. The dispute between those two approaches will be discussed at length in chapter 2.

However, there are certain actions that are forbidden whether one is a stockholder theorist or a stakeholder theorist. Neither theory would permit managers to violate our basic ethical principle: Normally put the interests of the client (the principal) ahead of your own interests. For instance, on either view managers are urged to avoid conflicts of interest.

▲ CONFLICTS OF INTEREST ▲

Often when a manager puts his or her own interest ahead of those he or she works for, it is because there is a conflict of interest. Two definitions of a conflict of interest are prominent in the philosophical literature. Michael Davis has defined conflict of interest as follows: "A person has a conflict of interest if, (a) he is in a relationship of trust with another requiring him to exercise judgment in that other's service and, (b) he has an interest tending to interfere with the proper exercise of that judgment."[4] Tom Beauchamp has proposed a similar definition. A conflict of interest occurs whenever there exists a conflict between a person's private or institutional gain and that same person's official duties in a position of trust.[5]

It is very difficult for managers to avoid the appearance of a conflict of interest. Almost every management decision will have an impact for good or ill on the personal fortunes of the manager. In law, managers are protected by the business judgment rule. The business judgment rule is a legal principle that assumes the manager is acting in the interests of the corporation in the day-to-day managing of the business. Under this rule, management error – even egregious error such as when Time Warner allowed itself to merge with AOL – is protected from a shareholder suit. Actions that are not protected by the business judgment rule are those that are self-serving.

You do not need a book on management ethics to know that enriching yourself at the expense of those who are paying your salary is wrong. And some behavior that reflects self-serving behavior is clearly wrong. For example, when a manager sets up a private individual consulting business that is in direct competition with the company he works for, he is violating a duty of loyalty and is involved in a straightforward conflict of interest. Other examples of conflicts of interest and unjust personal enrichment are more controversial, however. Few are as controversial as the amount of executive compensation.

EXCESSIVE COMPENSATION ▲

The CEOs and others occupying high management positions in the firm earn a lot of money. But the money they earn pales in light of the compensation they receive, usually in the form of stock options. Business ethicists have been criticizing executive compensation, almost from the beginning. But we were scorned as envious and ignorant of the market. As one critic of Norman Bowie pointed out at a public meeting: Managers incur risks that tenured professors do not and in large companies the lives of thousands depend on the quality of the decisions they make. The assumption was that executive managers earn their high salaries and thus deserve them.

But 20 years have passed since business ethicists and a few courageous executives such as Chuck Denny, former CEO of ADC Telecommunications, criticized the amount of executive compensation. Now even the most conservative business publications have joined the ranks of the business ethics critics. Every year *Fortune*, *Business Week*, and even the *Wall Street Journal* have articles noting the ever-rising gap between these executives and the rest of us. What follows, then, is a list of those executives who gave the most to the stockholders and those who gave the least. The situation has become so bad that in 2001, *Fortune* ran a separate feature account of excessive executive compensation entitled, "The Great CEO Pay Heist." In that account the writer refers to executive compensation as "highway robbery."

The numbers here are staggering. One of the baselines for tracking executive compensation is the gap between the pay of the average factory worker and the average CEO. This gap has risen steadily and consistently for over a decade, peaking in 2000 at 400 : 1, up from a ration of 42 : 1 in 1980.[6] Over the past two years, executive compensation has declined to the level of 1996.[7] As a result of this decline, the ratio of executive compensation to the compensation of the average factory worker declined to just over 200 : 1. However, it should be pointed out that the decline in compensation was due to the spectacular hits in pay and bonuses that some executives took. It should be noted that median pay for the 365 CEOs in the sample increased by 5.9 percent.[8] Similar data were found in the *Fortune* data set for 100 CEOs.[9] These data continue a long history. *Newsweek* from July 22, 2002, reports that executive pay is up 233 percent in a decade.

If that were not enough, many companies that had been under indictment for accounting scandals or other misdeeds have been the most egregious with respect to excessive compensation. Tyco is the pacesetter here. Tyco produced three of the top six earners in the 2002 *Fortune* list. Dennis Kozlowski, now under indictment for tax evasion, was among the six, so was his former CFO Mark Swartz, who made $136 million. Then to complete the trio, the person hired to clean up the scandal, Ed Breen, was paid $62 million. By the way the new CFO made $25 million, as did a Tyco division head.[10] As it went bankrupt, Asia Global Crossing forgave a $15 million loan plus giving a $2.75 million severance package to its CEO, but stopped severance pay to laid-off workers. Charles Conway, then CEO of Kmart, sought bankruptcy court approval for a $6.5 million bonus and forgiveness of a $5 million loan. Robert McGinn, fired one month before the start of a Securities and Exchange Commission (SEC) investigation, got a settlement that included $3.5 million plus $7 million in restricted stock sales and an annual pension of $870,000.

Actual salaries and bonuses are only part of the issue. The other part is stock options, which have become a very important part of an executive's compensation package. In the top 200 corporations, stock options equal 16 percent of all the outstanding shares. We will discuss other ethical issues with the widespread use of options below. Business continues to fight accounting reforms that would require businesses to report stock options as an expense. However, the Sarbanes–Oxley Act passed in July 2002 will outlaw some of the abuses discussed above and will allow the government to seize financial gains that have been achieved in violation of the law.

Nevertheless, there is an understandable reluctance to deal with these issues through the law. Attempts to do so have failed. *Fortune* has made the case persuasively:

> In 1989, Congress tries to cap golden parachutes by imposing an excise tax on payments 2.99 times base salary. Result: Companies make 2.99 the new minimum and cover any excise tax for execs. In 1992, Congress tries to shame CEO's by requiring better disclosure of their pay. Result: CEO's see how much everyone else is making and then try to get more. In 1993 Congress declares salaries over $1 million to be non tax-exempt. Result: Companies opt for huge stock option grants while upping most salaries to $1 million.[11]

We will continue to see instances of the law of unintended consequences as we discuss other attempts to regulate management ethics. Generally, ethicists support voluntary ethical restraint over legal regulation. But just what is it that is unfair or unjust about current executive compensation?

What is it about current executive compensation that has put the conservative business press into alliance with business ethicists? I think there are two reasons. First, there is little relation between results and compensation. When the company does well, executive compensation goes way up. When the company does poorly, executive compensation goes up. When times are good it is the result of the brilliant decisions of the CEO. When times are tough the fault is external circumstances over which the executives had little or no control. And since every company wants their executives to be above average (like all the children in Lake Wobegon) executive compensation spirals upward as each corporation tries to get or keep its executives above average.

But is that wrong? It is wrong if the argument for executive compensation is performance. High compensation that is not earned is not just. Even the editors of the *Wall Street Journal* accept that proposition.

The current compensation scheme is wrong for another reason. The true amount of compensation is kept hidden from the other stakeholders, especially the stockholders. This represents an abuse of what we shall call throughout this book *information asymmetry*. Information asymmetry occurs when one party in a relationship has information that another person or persons in the relationship does not have though they have a legal or moral right to that information. The amount of information that stockholders have a right to is determined by Generally Accepted Accounting Principles (GAAP), the reporting requirements of the SEC, as well as the reporting requirements of the various stock exchanges. How then is management able to keep information on executive compensation hidden from the investing public? The answer is options or what one writer for *Fortune* calls "the amazing stock option sleight of hand." Here is how it works. We must first realize that options are not free even though most companies refuse to treat them as an expense. By increasing the number of shares, the stake of existing shareholders in the company is reduced. Second, the company forgoes income when the options are offered at a low price to the executives. When the options are exercised, they become an expense that affects the bottom line, unless the company repurchases shares. Why would the cost of repurchase not show up? Because the Financial Accounting Standards Board (FASB) backed down when executives objected. How big a problem is this? The *Fortune* article reports on a study that shows that to keep shares from being watered down at the 436 large cap companies in 1999, the companies would have to spend $53 billion a year buying back their own stock – 13 percent of operating earnings – 51 percent for tech companies.[12] Generally speaking, the investing public is totally unaware of this potential liability, which could have a serious impact on future earnings.

The tide may be turning on stock options. Several companies, such as Coca-Cola, have agreed to treat stock options as an expense. There is great pressure on companies that have not done so to begin doing so. On July 8, 2003, Microsoft announced that employees would no longer receive stock options but would receive restricted stock instead.

If companies were required to list options as an expense, would this address the question of whether or not executive compensation is just? Complete transparency does not resolve the justice question. Rather, complete transparency is needed if we are to determine whether the current distribution of income – broadly defined – is just. If all the information about the costs of options were disclosed in a way that was easily available to the public, would they be considered just?

Let us also assume that in addition to being transparent they were also based strictly on performance. Would these two features be sufficient for us to say that current patterns of executive compensation are just? We think not.

The assumption is that when a company does well, it is the result of the work of a few executives at the top. Well, success is almost certainly due in part to them, but how much is due to them and how much is due to the efforts of those who work for them? Most of the productivity gains are going to the few executives at the top and as a result there is less for the other employees and there is also less for the stockholders. Some of the strongest critics of executive compensation are groups that are most interested in protecting the rights of stockholders. On the issue of executive compensation, there need be no disagreement between defenders of the financial rights of stockholders and defenders of the financial interests of the other stakeholders in addition to stockholders. The bottom line on this topic is that the current level of executive compensation cannot be justified.

One reason it cannot be justified is that there is a conflict of interest here. High executive salaries mean that there is less available for shareholders and other stakeholders. The members of the boards of directors that set compensation are, for the most part, corporate executives. It is in their interest that corporate salaries rise even though it is not in the interests of the stockholders. After all, for a CEO board member to challenge the salary of another CEO when that other CEO may well sit on your board, would be the height of imprudence. Also, there is a tendency for board members not to want the salary of their CEO to be below average. To allow that to happen would send an unwanted message that the company and the company's CEO are below average. All of this shows that CEO salaries are not mainly determined by the market but rather by other factors. What is needed is some theory of fairness to determine how the revenues of a firm should be divided among the stakeholders who contribute to making those revenues. In other words, in an ideal world, we could measure the contribution of each stakeholder to the success of the firm, subtract compensation received and end up with the profit. Stockholder theory says that all the profit belongs to the stockholders. Stakeholder theorists might argue that some of the "profit" should go to lower prices for customers and increased wages for employees. But no theory says that management ought to get as much of the profit as it can before distributing it to other stakeholders.

To be frank, we are not aware of any ethical theory that would justify the current level of executive compensation. The most likely theory is libertarianism. Libertarianism argues that freedom is an ultimate value and that exchanges or contracts freely entered into without coercion or deceit are morally valid. Some scholars, including many in finance, view a corporation as nothing more than a nexus of contracts.[13] Thus with this theory, high-level managers would be entitled to their high salaries, stock options, and other perks, if they resulted from contracts freely entered into without deception and fraud. It should be noted that most business ethicists find libertarianism to be flawed. Managers who are agents of the stockholders do not have actual contracts with their principals – the stockholders. The board of directors, which is supposed to make sure that managers manage in the interest of the corporation and the stockholders, has frequently failed miserably, as was seen in the Enron case. Many scholars argue that a corporation should not be understood as simply a nexus of contracts, and if these scholars are right it would be more difficult to apply libertarianism to the corporate setting.[14] Suppose a libertarian contractarian view of the corporation could survive critical scrutiny, even then the current compensation of many high-level executives could not be justified. Even on its own grounds, the present pattern of executive compensation cannot be justified because of the existence of deception and fraud in some cases. More generally, we have seen that managers have tried one device after another to keep the details of their compensation opaque. Libertarians would agree that a contract where one of the parties is not supplied with pertinent information is not a fair contract. Some political philosophers would even raise issues with coercion. For example, in times of high unemployment, employees accept whatever job they can get. Whether acceptance of a contract in dire straits is coercion and thus unfair is a matter of great controversy in political philosophy. We cannot go into the details of that discussion here. Suffice it to say that the revelations regarding executive compensation cast into doubt whether the compensation is based on transparent contracts with stockholders, free of deception and fraud.

Utilitarianism will not help either. Utilitarianism urges that we either take that action (Act Utilitarianism) or follow that rule (Rule Utilitarianism) that leads to the greatest balance of good for all those affected. Central to utilitarianism is something called the law of diminishing marginal utility. The first ice-cream cone on a hot summer day has high utility. A second one has positive utility but not as much as the first. Each additional ice-cream cone has less utility than the ice-cream cone that preceded it. Suppose we apply the law of diminishing marginal utility to compensation itself. Each extra dollar of compensation has utility but not as much as the dollar of compensation that preceded it. Thus, it would increase total utility if compensation were shifted from those who were most compensated (corporate executives) to those who were less compensated (the average factory worker.) One way to avoid this conclusion is to argue that the rich have more expensive tastes than those less well off and greater utility results when those expensive tastes are satisfied. However, this is not a position that the rich are willing to publicly advocate – a necessary condition for any valid ethical principle, as we shall see.

Another more promising response is to argue that a utilitarian analysis of compensation requires more than applying the law of diminishing marginal utility to money. Social good results when factors like skill and effort are rewarded. Surely that is correct. However, what the exhaustive catalogue of abuse shows is that current compensation cannot be based on the greater skill or effort of managers. If the utilitarian case is to hold, it must be on the basis of the skill, effort, and productivity of managers. So far that case has not been made; the present distribution of managerial compensation seems to be more the result of self-serving behavior than traits that benefit the public good.

Probably the best theory to evaluate executive compensation is some version of justice theory. After all, we are looking for the fair means of dividing up the profits from the cooperative efforts of the various stakeholders in a business. The late John Rawls developed a procedure for determining principles of justice. Although he specifically limited his method to deriving principles for a just society, his approach may be helpful here. Suppose all the various stakeholders were gathered together in one spot to decide on how the income from a firm should be divided up. Thus representatives from labor, capital, management, and the local community would all be present.[15] Suppose next that representatives of the various stakeholders were to act as if they did not know to which stakeholder group they belonged. In Rawls' terminology, they would be behind a veil of ignorance. How would such a group of representatives from the various stakeholder groups choose? There is no reason to believe they would choose the current system where so many of the productivity gains have gone to management.

Rawls argued that people behind the veil of ignorance did have considerable basic knowledge – knowledge of human nature and the basic laws of psychology and economics. In these situations Rawls believed the parties behind the veil could unanimously agree to two basic principles of justice – the liberty principle and the difference principle. The liberty principle states: "Each person has an equal right to the most extensive basic liberty compatible with a similar liberty for others." The difference principle states that "Social and economic inequalities are to be arranged so that they are both (a) reasonably expected to be to everyone's advantage and (b) attached to positions and offices open to all."[16] We believe that stakeholders behind the veil of interest would adopt principle 1 and part (b) of principle 2. What is more problematic is whether they would choose part (a) where any inequalities must work to the benefit of all. Our doubts about whether part (a) would be unanimously accepted show how difficult it is to really step behind the veil of ignorance. Our own brand of capitalism already has a long-established history and it is hard to imagine theories of compensation that are too divorced from our own experience. Suppose we allow knowledge of our legal system and economic system to be outside the veil of ignorance. Our best guess is that stakeholders would agree that stockholders are entitled to a certain historical percentage of profit traditionally defined. However, profit that results from productivity gains, through improved technology or increased worker efficiency, should be split more or less evenly to the various stakeholder groups or distributed according to objective measures of the contribution of each stakeholder group to the "abnormal" increase in profits. All this sounds indeterminate and so it is. But we think it is still more reasonable than the myth of the strong CEO who single-handedly turns a company around. A CEO does not do that by him- or herself.

Finally and simply put, CEOs and other executives have been too greedy. As *Fortune* put it, "Have They No Shame?"[17] The accusations of greed are numerous, but getting a handle on greed requires tying the notion to ethical theory. Accusations of greed imply that a person has a vice and thus a character flaw. The ethical theory that serves as the historical basis for defining virtues and good character is Aristotelian ethics. Aristotle argued that a virtue represents a mean between two extremes or deficiencies.[18] Thus courage is the mean between rashness and cowardice. Aristotle did not discuss greed per se, but he did recognize the virtues of generosity and magnificence. Generosity is concerned with wealth and is the mean between the vices of wastefulness and lack of generosity. The generous person is concerned with giving rather than taking, is not overly concerned with wealth accumulation, and his or her attitude toward accumulation is neither mean nor wasteful. Magnificence is the virtue of generosity writ large. Aristotle says that magnificence is a virtue like generosity that is concerned with wealth but that it extends only to people who have a lot of wealth. Magnificence is the virtue between the vices of excess and stinginess. The vulgar person spends more than is necessary. Think of Kozlowski, the former CEO of Tyco. The stingy person does not spend enough. Think of the dinner party that resembles a spartan health spa. Some of Aristotle's analysis captures what we mean by greedy. Having a lot of money does not make a person greedy. Bill Gates is one of the world's richest men, but Gates has been both generous and magnificent. But many highly paid managers are viewed by the public as both living in excess and as being ungenerous. Both of these are Aristotelian vices.

Despite the usefulness of Aristotle's virtue ethics here, we wish to emphasize our central point. Managers are agents either of the stockholders or the stakeholders. They are entitled to fair compensation as determined by the market. But excessive compensation is morally wrong and is judged to be so both by moral theory and by business pundits in the business press.

▲ PROBLEMS OF EGO AND POWER ▲

Executives also can fail to meet their obligations as managers by becoming corrupted by the power of the office. Executives have high status and high compensation. People naturally tend to defer to them and if they are successful they tend to think they can manage other organizations, such as universities or not-for-profit companies. Executives are particularly likely to fall victim to the vice of hubris. One of the classic sociological studies of a major corporation, *Moral Mazes* by Robert Jackall, has shown that managers are not working diligently for the shareholders or for other corporate stakeholders but rather are constantly plotting to stay in power. Middle managers spend their time trying to be on the winning team and then aping the behavior of the person they think will be most successful. Sometimes this goes as far as dressing like the person one is emulating and even adopting their mannerisms.

In addition, managers are always seeking more and more perks which only adds to the moral issue surrounding excessive compensation. The June 12, 2003, *Wall Street Journal* reports on the plush pads that companies provide their CEOs. The plush pad might be a condo unit in New York that the CEO gets rent free or at a greatly reduced rent. Alternatively it might be a lavish home that the CEO purchases using a loan from the company.[19] Frequently, these perks are not reported as personal income to the Internal Revenue Service. Even more frequently these perks are not reported to the shareholders. Here is what the *Wall Street Journal* reporters Motoko Rich and Sheila Muto found:

> General Electric Co., for example, owns four apartments for its officials in a luxury building at the base of Central Park in New York City. Rayovac Corp. bought a home assessed at $832,200 for its chief executive in Westport Wis. E*Trade Group Inc. owns an expensive house in California's Silicon Valley used by its former president. And many companies including Mattel Inc. and Chiron Corp. have loaned their CEOs millions to buy homes – and then sometimes have forgiven the loans.[20]

Moreover, the perks do not necessarily end with retirement. Consider the case of Geoffrey Bible, recently retired from Philip Morris. In return for being available for occasional consulting, Bible will get the following for life:

1. An office near his home and a secretary.
2. An unlimited phone-calling card.
3. Two cell phones and two fax machines plus the cost of maintenance.
4. Security at his home and vacation home.

5. Access to the corporate plane, dining room, and gym.
6. A company car and driver or a car allowance up to $100,000 a year.
7. Up to $15,000 a year in financial advisory services.[21]

When questioned by *Business Week*, a Philip Morris spokesperson said that the company had done in-depth research and that the package is comparable to that of other executives.[22] If true, we can simply question the morality of standard practice. Since managers are agents of the corporation, how can such perks be justified?

Gray areas

Although excessive compensation, benefits, and perks have received the bulk of the attention in this chapter, there are other management practices that also appear to benefit managers at the expense of the stockholders and on occasion other corporate stakeholders. We put these practices in a gray area because these practices may be legitimate in certain contexts as well. Notice that our concerns about compensation were about abuse or excess. We now turn to certain managerial practices and evaluate the practices themselves. Each case must be judged on its merits, but there are general principles we can use to determine whether an actual case is justified or not.

▲ POISON PILLS AND OTHER ▲ ANTI-TAKEOVER DEFENSES

Not all issues of managers' role morality are clear-cut. Enriching oneself at the company's expense is a violation of the obligations of an agent. Some actions that are morally suspect are not done to enrich oneself but might be done to benefit the shareholders, the very people who are the principals that manager-agents serve.

The history of corporate takeovers presents an issue of this type. The raider always argues that management is not living up to its responsibility to manage in the best interest of the stockholders. That is why the stock is undervalued, the raider argues. In the language of this chapter, managers are not living up to their role obligations; the raider and his team could do a better job at managing the corporation than the current management team, it is argued. If it were only that simple, and sometimes it is. On occasion, a hostile takeover might be justified on the grounds that the company really is badly run, and it becomes clear when the takeover succeeds that the raider could indeed run the company better than the management it displaced. Given the function of management, when that occurs it can be said that it is a good thing.

Management has put in place a number of defenses to protect itself from hostile takeovers. Staggered board terms and super-majority voting rules are fairly straightforward. Other defenses have more colorful names: poison pills, scorched earth policy, Pac-man defense, and white knights. The raiders claim that such defenses are morally illegitimate because they are simply designed to keep management in power. Attempts to stay in power are in violation of management's role obligations to increase the wealth of stock-holders. If that were the whole story, anti-takeover defenses would not be a gray area; they would be wrong.

Anti-takeover defenses represent a gray area because management can often legitimately argue that the anti-takeover defenses are not there to benefit them but are there to benefit other stakeholders, such as the employees and the community. It is also argued that they protect the long-term investor from the arbitrageur. In the late 1980s takeovers were all the rage. The Dayton Hudson Corporation (now Target) even appealed to the Minnesota legislature to pass an anti-takeover bill to help Dayton Hudson in its struggle with Hafts, the former owners of Dart, a drug store chain on the East Coast. History has shown that the Dayton Hudson management in place at the time was almost certainly better able to manage Dayton Hudson in the long run. In addition to Minnesota, many states now have laws that allow companies to take the interests of all stakeholders into account when considering a takeover bid. In the summer of 2003, Oracle launched a hostile takeover bid for PeopleSoft. Many have charged that the tactics of Oracle CEO Larry Ellison have been unfair and many of PeopleSoft's customers have taken its side, indicating that Oracle ownership would not be of benefit to them. On moral grounds, some anti-takeover defenses are not undertaken to entrench and protect management, but sometimes they are. When such defenses are used simply to keep management in power, then they are wrong. However, when they are used to defend the long-term financial health of the company or to protect the interests of employees, customers, and the local community, as was the case with Dayton Hudson and PeopleSoft, then they will be morally permissible.

Managing earnings

During the accounting and reporting scandals of 2002, a number of practices that were legal were called into question. Some companies, such as General Electric, had an uncanny record of always having their reported earnings meet their estimated earnings. There always seemed to be an expense or a revenue that was available when needed. For many years the market had rewarded GE's success, but in 2002 the success had the smell of manipulation. GE's stock price fell nearly 40 percent. If the quarterly reports are to give a transparent picture of that quarter, it seems that managed earnings are ethically inappropriate. Managed earnings do help managers because they are rewarded when the estimates of earnings targets are hit. But the current stockholders gain as well as the stock price is bid up. The stock market is very responsive to whether management meets its quarterly estimates. If they meet or exceed estimates, the stock usually rises sharply – at least in the short run. On the other hand, if the quarterly estimate is not met the stock usually falls sharply – at least in the short run. If managers are agents of the stockholders, what is wrong with managed earnings when it is the stockholders that benefit, even if managers do as well? The answer is that an efficient market works best when information is accurate and timely – when there is transparency. That is why the auditing firms have rules that forbid moving expenses and income to quarters where they are not really booked. Managed earnings is an attempt to "game the system" and in that way mislead the investing public. However, given the focus of investors on the quarterly numbers, one can understand why management is tempted to manage earnings.

▲ A WORD ABOUT CORPORATE ▲ GOVERNANCE AND REGULATION

The starting point of management ethics is that managers fulfill their role obligations to their clients or principals. Even though there is some dispute regarding who the principals are, all perspectives agree that it is wrong for managers to enrich themselves at the expense of their clients. Regrettably, many managers have done just that. We have documented this malfeasance throughout this chapter. What is to be done? Obviously managers ought to be ethical; they ought to fulfill their role obligations. They ought not to exploit their clients in ways that enable them to enrich themselves. However, in the face of such widespread unethical behavior, society has turned to law and the reform of corporate governance. Congress passed the Sarbanes–Oxley Act in July of 2002 in an attempt to make some abuses illegal. In addition it authorized better regulation of managers by stipulating how the board of directors should function.[23] By insisting that a certain percentage of the board consist of independent directors, Congress is trying to make the board more independent of management. Although we think that much of the law is laudable, a detailed discussion of it and the agencies it created is beyond the scope of this book. An unethical manager will always seek a way around the law. Our task is to spell out the duties and obligations of the moral manager. Once that is clear, each manager must determine for him- or herself whether to be ethical or not. How to ensure that managers make the right choice is more a matter of public policy than management ethics.

Does role morality trump ordinary morality?

One common defense when someone in a position or role violates ordinary moral norms is that the obligations of the role trump ordinary morality. The most common defense of this type is the defense given of the legal practice of zealous advocacy. Lawyers argue that it is morally permissible for them to zealously defend a client even when the lawyer knows the client is guilty. It is assumed that the prosecutors will prosecute zealously and thus the system works best when each lawyer presents the most zealous defense possible for his or her client. In politics, it is usually assumed that statesmen are permitted to lie if by lying the citizens of the state are better protected. The same goes for torturing prisoners or denying them moral or legal rights. One thinks of the war against terrorism. The claim that the role morality of the statesman trumps ordinary morality in these cases goes by the name of "the Problem of Dirty Hands." Whether the obligations of one's role ever trump ordinary morality is a controversial matter.

Does the pursuit of profit for stockholders allow managers to violate law and morality in doing so? We think not. Most business ethicists, even when defending the stockholder theory of profitability, do not allow the struggle for profits to justify illegal or clearly unethical behavior. Very few business professors or business people have tried to make the case either. Theodore Levitt defended certain kinds of deceptive advertising, when the advertising was used to make us feel better about ourselves. Albert Carr argued that business ethics was different from the ethics of ordinary morality and more like the ethics of poker. For Carr business did have an ethics; it was just less stringent than regular morality. Neither Levitt nor Carr made the stronger claim that understanding the function of business and the resulting role morality of the manager exhausted the ethics of business.

There are good philosophical reasons for arguing that role morality cannot be the last word in management ethics. First, role morality may not give answers when management has obligations to two or more corporate stakeholders and the interests of the stakeholders are in conflict. Higher wages for employees versus no price increase for consumers is a standard example. In order to settle such conflicts, the adherent of role morality must reference a higher morality outside role morality to settle the issue. Second, there is the problem of conflicts among roles. Many managers are also parents and spouses. Being a parent or a spouse brings with it its own role obligations. How is one to decide which role takes precedence when there is a conflict between, or even among, roles? Stories of managers who sacrifice their families for their careers are legion. One cannot appeal to role morality to settle such conflicts. One needs to appeal to an ethical theory. Finally, what gives role morality even limited authority? Why does the fact that one occupies various roles matter morally? To answer that question one appeals to traditional moral theories like utilitarianism, a theory of justice, or a theory like Kant's that emphasizes purity of motive, consistency, and respect for persons. In summary, role morality cannot be the final justification in ethics because role morality, with its unique set of role obligations, needs itself to be justified.

▲ CONCLUSION ▲

In this chapter we have established that it is wrong for the manager to put his or her interests ahead of the interests of the person he or she works for. Prima facie, the manager is the agent of the stockholders. To act in one's own interest at the expense of the owners is thus unethical. But what if one acts in the interests of others with a stake in the firm at the expense of the owners? Is that morally wrong? In that instance you are not putting your own interests ahead of the owners, but rather arguing that another stakeholder has a morally relevant interest that trumps in that case. Whether the manager should manage exclusively for the stockholder or should manage for all the stakeholders is the subject of the next chapter.

▲ NOTES ▲

1. Adolf A. Berle and Gardiner C. Means, *The Modern Corporation and Private Property* (New York: Macmillan, 1932).
2. We are indebted to Robert Frederick for this argument.
3. We admit that the existence of health maintenance organizations (HMOs) has complicated the role of doctors who work for them.
4. Michael Davis, "University Research and the Wages of Commerce," *Journal of College and University Law* 18 (1991), pp. 29–39.
5. Tom L. Beauchamp, "Ethical Issues in Funding and Monitoring University Research," *Business and Professional Ethics Journal* 11 (1992), pp. 5–16.
6. Amy Borrus, "A Battle Royal Against Regal Paychecks," *Business Week* (February 24, 2003).
7. "Executive Pay," *Business Week* (April 21, 2003), pp. 86–90.
8. Ibid.
9. Jerry Useem, "Have They No Shame?" *Fortune* (April 29, 2003), pp. 57–64.
10. Ellen E Scultz and Theo Francis, "Executives Get Pension Security While Plans for Workers Falter," *Wall Street Journal* (April 24, 2003), pp. A1, A10.
11. Useem, "Have They No Shame?" p. 59.
12. Quoted from "The Amazing Stock Option Sleight of Hand," *Fortune* (June 25, 2001).
13. See for example Michael C. Jensen and William H. Meckling, "Theory of the Firm: Managerial Behavior, Agency Costs, and Ownership Structure," *Journal of Financial Economics* 3 (1976), p. 310.
14. For an alternative view, see R. Edward Freeman and Robert A. Phillips, "Stakeholder Theory: A Libertarian Defense," *Business Ethics Quarterly* 12 (2002), pp. 331–49.
15. A Rawlsian approach to stakeholder management has been suggested by R. Edward Freeman, "A Stakeholder Theory of the Modern Corporation," pp. 66–76 in *Ethical Theory and Business*, 5th edition, ed. Tom L. Beauchamp and Norman E. Bowie (Upper Saddle River, NJ: Prentice Hall, 1997). This article has been reprinted in the 6th and 7th editions as well.
16. John Rawls, *A Theory of Justice* (Cambridge, MA.: Harvard University Press, 1971).

17. Ibid., pp. 60–1.
18. Aristotle's theory of virtue and character development is found in his *Nicomachean Ethics*. The account of the virtues of generosity and magnificence is taken from Aristotle, *Nicomachean Ethics*, Terrence Irwin, trans. (Indianapolis: Hackett, 1985), pp. 85–97.
19. Most of these loans have now been outlawed by the 2002 Sarbanes–Oxley Act.
20. Motoko Rich and Sheila Muto, "The CEO's Plush Pad," *Wall Street Journal* (June 12, 2002), p. B1.
21. "At Philip Morris, Perks For Life," *Business Week* (July 15, 2002).
22. Ibid.
23. The act also created a Public Board to oversee the auditing firms and the accountants.

chapter two

Stockholder Management or Stakeholder Management

▲ THE STOCKHOLDER THEORY OF ▲ MANAGERIAL OBLIGATION

The orthodox view in business schools, particularly in departments of finance and accounting, is that the manager is an agent for the stockholders. He or she works for them and should do their bidding. Their bidding is profits and thus the purpose of a manager is to increase the wealth of the stockholders. The Nobel Prize winner Milton Friedman is most closely associated with that view. He has said:

> There is one and only one social responsibility of business – to use its resources and engage in activities designed to increase its profits as long as it stays within the rules of the game, which is to say, engages in free and open competition without deception or fraud.

And again:

> In a free enterprise, private-property system, a corporate executive is an employee of the owners of the business. He has direct responsibility to his employers. That responsibility is to conduct the business in accordance with their desires, which generally will be to make as much money as possible while conforming to the basic rules of the society, both those embodied in law and those embodied in ethical custom.[1]

It is important to note that Friedman is not saying that managers ought to maximize profits even if that is done in an unethical way. Friedman is very clear in saying that managers have a duty not to use deception and fraud in business. Business managers should engage in open competition. Price collusion would be a moral wrong for

Friedman. Business managers ought to follow the law and they ought to obey the ethical customs embedded in society.

This is an important point to make since some writers have taken an overly permissive moral view while subscribing to the orthodox theory. Theodore Levitt, a former editor of the *Harvard Business Review*, has defended various deceptive practices in advertising. On the basis that consumers want to be deceived he wrote the following in 1970:

> Rather than deny that distortion and exaggeration exist in advertising, in this article I shall argue that embellishment and distortion are among advertisement's legitimate and socially desirable purposes; and that illegitimacy in advertising consists only of falsification with larcenous intent ... But the consumer suffers from an old dilemma. He wants "truth" but he also wants and needs alleviating imagery and tantalizing promise of the advertiser and designer.[2]

We believe there are several mistakes in this argument. The first is a factual mistake. We do not believe that people want to be deceived although we certainly do not deny that they are deceived. The second mistake is that even if consumers want to be deceived, it does not mean that they should be deceived – especially when there are good moral arguments against deception. Third, Levitt seems to assume that advertisers should deceive consumers for their own good. What is the justification for this kind of paternalism?

Yet another overly permissive adherent of the orthodox view is the late Albert Carr. Carr argued that business has its own morality that is different from ordinary morality. Carr presents an argument of the kind we discussed in chapter 1, where it is alleged that the role morality of business trumps ordinary morality. Carr said this in 1968:

> Poker's own brand of ethics is different from the ethical ideals of civilized human relationships. The game calls for distrust of the other fellow. It ignores the claim of friendship. Cunning deception and concealment of one's strength and intentions, not kindness and open heartedness, are vital in poker. No one thinks any the worse of poker on that account. And no one should think worse of the game of business because the standards of right and wrong differ from the prevailing traditions of morality in our society.

Carr continues:

That most businessmen are not indifferent to ethics in their private lives, everyone will agree. My point is that in their office lives they cease to be private citizens; they become game players who must be guided by a somewhat different set of standards ... The golden rule, for all its value as an ideal for society, is simply not feasible as a guide for business. A good part of the time the businessman is trying to do unto others as he hopes others will not do unto him.[3]

As with the argument by Levitt, there are several errors in this argument. First, the game analogy is a poor analogy. People choose to play poker and to accept the risks of that game. They do not choose to participate in business – at least not in any real sense. Nearly all of us need to participate in the workforce if we want to live. Second, in poker everyone knows that bluffing is an acceptable move. That is not the normal case in business, although it may be in the selling of homes and the buying of cars. But that is not how it is with the financial reports of publicly held corporations. People do not expect managers to bluff about their financial reports, although it is now clear that many do. Third, one needs a compelling argument to claim that the moral norms of a practice trump the norms of ordinary morality. Carr provides no such argument. Moreover, in chapter 1 we presented several arguments why in most cases role morality cannot trump ordinary morality. Indeed, how could the making of money justify deception, when the lack of deception, as we saw, is required to make money?

Moreover, Robert Frederick has an argument to show that both Levitt and Carr must presuppose the ordinary morality, specifically the rule against lying and deception, which they deny. Frederick refers to this argument as the "so what" argument. Both Levitt and Carr argue that business is a game played by its own rules. Now suppose one of the players violates one of the rules of the business game. There are two possibilities. The first is that no one cares that a rule has been violated. In that case it makes no sense to claim that business is played by rules. Most likely however, the rule violator would be challenged. On what basis would that challenge be made? Presumably either the rule violator had promised to abide by the business rules and in violating them had broken a promise, or breaking them is unfair or unjust. The rule violator is free-riding on those who are following the rules of the business game. However, appeals to keeping promises or to fairness are appeals to ordinary moral rules. So either there are no rules to the business game or adherence to the rules of the business game presupposes adherence to the rules of ordinary morality. Thus, Carr's argument fails.

We now conclude that Friedman's position does not require that managers violate basic ethical norms in order to enhance the wealth of the stockholders. The ethical norms of ordinary morality apply. Let us now move on to see how an adherent of the orthodox position would argue for resolving conflicts among the corporate stakeholders.

Suppose the orthodox view is correct. How does the manager accomplish this goal? How does he or she fulfill her obligations and responsibilities to stockholders? Answering that question is the true challenge of ethical management. This is because the success of a firm depends on many other groups of people, called stakeholders. Traditionally these stakeholder groups include the stockholders, employees, customers, suppliers, the local community, and yes, even the managers.[4] Since meeting the interests of the stakeholders is necessary for the success of the firm, then even on the orthodox view, profitability depends on the cooperation of the stakeholders. Thus, even on the orthodox view a manager can only fulfill his or her obligations to stockholders if the needs and desires of the other stakeholders are met. But since the needs and desires of the stakeholders often conflict, carrying out the responsibilities of management becomes a very complex task. Given the myriad conflicting interests, there is a corresponding myriad of ethical issues.

In the previous chapter we discussed conflicts of interest where the manager put his or her own personal self-interest ahead of the interests of others to whom he or she had an obligation. But a conflict of interest can occur whenever one puts the interest of another ahead of those whose interests should be served. If the manager is the agent of the stockholders and has a fiduciary duty to them, then if the manager puts the interest of another stakeholder, such as the employees or the community, ahead of the interests of the stockholders, one has a conflict of interest. On the other hand, if the manager is not solely the agent of the stockholder but has obligations to all the corporate stakeholders, then he or she is faced with the task of balancing conflicting interests rather than with a conflict of interest. In either case, one of the major moral issues faced by the manager is how conflicts should be resolved in the interests of stockholders and other stakeholders. How ought these conflicts to be resolved?

The orthodox theorist might think there is a simple answer to that question: since the manager is an agent of the stockholders any conflict must be settled in the interests of the stockholders. Long run or short run? The answer to that question is tremendously important for two reasons: First, some stockholders are in for the long term, but many others are in it for the short term only. That is why the quarterly results are so important on Wall Street. Second, always giving priority to the stockholders may well hurt stockholders in the long run. If you cut the cost of employees by increasing the workload or reducing benefits, you can have a positive short-term impact on the bottom line. But when scarce skilled workers are your employees, then frustrating their needs and desires in order to increase stockholder wealth in the short run will only hurt stockholders in the long run. Specifically it will hurt those stockholders who are in it for the long haul or stockholders who buy when those who benefit by the present decision sell out. What is hurt is long-term stockholder wealth in the aggregate.[5] Thus, we need to ask, should the interests of the long-term stockholder or the short-term arbitrageur take precedence? This is a very difficult question to answer. Some would avoid answering the question because they insist that all stockholders should be treated alike. Most adherents of the orthodox view take that position. But the position is seldom argued for. One could argue that the justification for market capitalism is its efficiency and that stockholders who are in it for the short term promote the efficiency of markets. Even if that were true, moral philosophers who are not utilitarian would not be persuaded. The issue in this case is whether priority should be put on the short term or the long term. When phrased in this way, you can clearly see that a choice involves winners and losers. On grounds of fairness and justice, why should the stockholder who has been loyal to the firm and is committed to a long-term investment in the firm be sacrificed to the short-term arbitrageur who simply wants to make a quick buck?

▲ THE STAKEHOLDER THEORY OF ▲ MANAGERIAL OBLIGATION

R. Edward Freeman is most closely associated with the view that management has a fiduciary duty to all its stakeholders and that the interests of the stockholders ought not to have priority over the interests of the other stakeholders. Freeman contends that management bears a fiduciary relationship to all stakeholders and that the task of the manager is to balance the competing claims of the various stakeholders:

> My thesis is that I can revitalize the concept of managerial capitalism by replacing the notion that managers have a duty to stockholders with the concept that managers bear a fiduciary relationship to stakeholders. Stakeholders are those groups who have a stake in or claim on the firm.[6]

Freeman distinguishes between a narrow use of the term "stakeholder" and a wider use of the term. On the narrow definition, stakeholders are those groups who are vital to the survival and success of the firm. On Freeman's account these are the owners, employees, customers, managers, suppliers, and the local community. On the wider definition, stakeholders are any group that affects or is affected by the firm.[7] In his own analysis, Freeman uses the narrow definition. We will follow Freeman in our analysis here.

Freeman admits that the law would need to change if his view were to prevail. However, he provides many examples where the law, over the past 50 or more years, has evolved to erode the rights of stockholders over other stakeholders. Profit has been circumscribed by a series of regulations over the past several decades. As we noted in chapter 1, several states have passed laws that specifically allow managers to take into account the interests of other stakeholder groups when considering whether to accept a takeover or leveraged buyout. These states permit companies chartered in those states to consider the impact of a hostile takeover on corporate stakeholders narrowly defined. One state, Pennsylvania, requires that the impact on stakeholders be considered.

How does a manager who manages from a stakeholder perspective make decisions? In Freeman's view, the stakeholder manager should operate on a normative core of fair contracts. This contract language is shared in common with a standard view that the firm is a nexus of contracts.[8] However, Freeman adds a normative or moral dimension to the contract language. The contracts among the various stakeholders must be fair. Given all the competing notions of fairness, how can we reach a consensus on what counts as a fair contract? Freeman borrows a device from John Rawls that we introduced in chapter 1. Freeman adapts Rawls' device of the original position under a veil of ignorance to answer that question. Suppose all the stakeholders had to unanimously agree with the basic principles for managing the firm. Moreover, they had to agree on these principles not knowing which stakeholder they would be. In other words, they would not know if they were in the stockholder group or the employee group with respect to any particular firm.[9]

Freeman believes that stakeholders operating under this condition would in fact agree to six principles, or ground rules as he calls them. The principle of entry and exit means that the corporation must have clearly defined entry, exit, and renegotiation conditions that enable any stakeholder to know when a contract exists and is valid. Then a stakeholder can decide whether he or she wants to be covered by this kind of contract. He or she also knows the rules for exiting the contract and for negotiating how the contract should apply to ever changing situations. The governance principle stipulates that procedures for changing the rules must be adopted by unanimous consent. Unanimity is required because stakeholders do not know which stakeholder they will be so they will seek governance rules that protect them all. That is why they will insist on unanimity. The third principle is the principle of externalities which states that any contract between A and B that imposes a cost on C makes C a party to the contract. Again, this principle makes sense under a veil of ignorance constraint. The fourth principle, "the principle of contracting costs," says that all parties to the contract must share in the cost of contracting. Behind a veil of ignorance, adoption of this principle seems obvious as a principle of self-defense and of fairness. The fifth principle is the agency principle that states that the manager must serve the interests of all the stakeholders. Here Freeman accepts a fundamental proposition of finance-based capitalism. Both Freeman and Michael Jensen would agree that the manager is an agent. As a result, both agree that the manager has role-related obligations. However, for Freeman the manager is an agent for more than the shareholders. The final principle of limited immortality says the corporation should be managed so that it can continue to serve the interests of stakeholders through time.

Although the stakeholder theory is not as well developed and rigorous as the classical stockholder theory, it has, nonetheless, proven highly successful in the marketplace. Many – indeed one might now say most – corporations at least speak the language of stakeholder theory even if they do not always practice it. Stakeholder language is also a part of a number of international agreements. The Caux Roundtable Principles for Business are explicitly based on and organized around the obligations that the manager owes to the various corporate stakeholders. Ewald Kist, CEO of ING group, spoke of his company as follows at the Georgetown Business Ethics Institute:

> We are a stakeholder driven company. We want to treat all the stakeholders in a balanced way ... We have clients, employees, shareholders and we have society. Our stakeholders watch us closely and critically, so we have to earn our license to operate on a day-to-day basis from our clients and all our business relationships. This is what is meant by the famous "people, planet, profit" also known as the triple bottom line.[10]

In Europe the environment has been added as a stakeholder – some have called it the silent stakeholder. Stakeholder notions have been incorporated in the notion of management for sustainability, where sustainability is measured by triple bottom-line accounting. Under this rubric, managers have a moral obligation to ensure the financial health of the organization, to protect the environment, and to behave in a socially responsible way. We shall have more to say about sustainability and triple bottom-line accounting in chapter 6. We believe that Europe is ahead of the United States in the implementation of stakeholder theory at the corporate level.

▲ CRITICISMS OF THE TWO THEORIES ▲

Despite its success in the marketplace of ideas, those who are adherents of the orthodox stockholder-oriented theory have roundly criticized the stakeholder theory. These critics point out that stakeholder theory greatly complicates management – especially if one claims, as Freeman does, that management has a fiduciary obligation to all stakeholders. The critics also point out that the wide concept of the stakeholder is too wide and that the narrow concept is too narrow. If one takes into account anyone affected by the firm, that turns management into an impossible task. Competitors and the customers of competitors are affected by the actions of a firm. People who see the advertisements and are moved to either enthusiastic approval or disgust are affected. On the other hand, if the narrow view is accepted along with the six stakeholder classes suggested by Freeman, then the number of stakeholders is too few. Recall, under the narrow definition any group whose existence is necessary to the success or survival of the firm is a stakeholder.

Government then becomes a stakeholder, since it punishes by civil or criminal law those who violate the rules of the game. It also provides infrastructure in the form of roads, police, fire, a stable monetary supply, etc. These are necessary for the survival of the firm and thus the government that provides them is a stakeholder. Some of this is captured in regarding the local community as stakeholder, but surely not all of it. The media and non-governmental organizations (NGOs), when they take an adversarial position with respect to a firm, can certainly undermine the firm's success. Should not the media and NGOs be considered stakeholders as well? Until these issues are settled the concept of a "stakeholder" is fuzzy and confused. This is especially annoying for the orthodox supporters of stockholder theory who correctly claim that profitability and shareholder wealth have reasonably fixed meanings and can be measured. Stakeholder theory also suffers from a priority problem. Since the interests of the stakeholders invariably clash, you need some way to determine under what conditions which stakeholders get priority. However, as the critics point out, there has been almost no progress in settling this issue. Thus, stakeholder theory is criticized as being conceptually ambiguous and impractical to implement.

Despite these difficulties for stakeholder theory, the stockholder theory has a few issues of its own. First, critics attack the functionalist defense of stockholder theory that was given at the beginning of this chapter. They argue that profits are not the purpose of the firm, but rather a condition of its future existence. That something is necessary for the existence of X does not show that it is the purpose of X. If we do not have air, food, and water, we die, but it is not the purpose of human beings to consume air, food, and water. (Admittedly, a few human beings behave that way with respect to food.) It is important to note that a number of successful managers understand this point exactly. George Merck II said it this way:

> I want to express the principles which we in our company have endeavored to live up to ... Here is how it sums up. We try to remember that medicine is for the patient. We try never to forget that medicine is for the people. It is not for profits. The profits follow, and if we have remembered that, they have never failed to appear. The better we have remembered it the larger they have been.[11]

And John Young, chief executive of Hewlett Packard from 1976 to 1992, put it this way:

Yes profit is a cornerstone of what we do – it is a measure of our contribution and a means of self-financed growth – but it has never been the point in and of itself. The point in fact is to win and winning is judged in the eye of the customer and by doing something you can be proud of. There is symmetry of logic in this. If we provide real satisfaction to real customers – we will be profitable.[12]

Basically, what the adherents of the stakeholder theory can say is that managers do have a moral obligation to make sure that the firm is profitable, just as parents have a moral obligation to make sure that their children have sufficient food, clothing, and shelter to survive. But the purpose of parenthood is not to provide food, clothing, and shelter; a parent who did simply that rather than provide the emotional support and love as well would be morally deficient as a parent. By analogy the same holds true of a corporation. Making a profit is only one of the moral obligations that a manager has. There is a lot more to it than that. And the "lot more to it" is managing to serve the interests of all the corporate stakeholders.

In addition, critics of the orthodox stockholder view believe the moral arguments given on behalf of the stockholder view are fatally flawed. One argument for the orthodox view is that the share-owners are owners of the company and as owners they have a property right to the profits. But the shareholders do not own the corporation in the way that you own your car. Normally, if you own something it is under your control. However, as Berle and Means pointed out in the 1930s, there is a separation between the share-holders who technically own the firm and the managers who control the daily operating of it. The shareholders have little direct control over the management of the firm. Indeed, as mentioned in chapter 1, ordinary business decisions are not subject to shareholders' deriva-tive suits because managers are protected by the business judgment rule. That rule, which is a central tenet of corporate law, says that shareholders cannot second-guess management in the normal exercise of the business even if the decisions of the managers have bad financial consequences.

We would not want to push this argument too far. It is one thing to say that the stockholders do not "own" the firm in the standard way. It would be quite another to say that their ownership does not create obligations on the part of management to manage the firm in their interests. This leads to the second argument for the orthodox view. The managers are employed as agents of the stockholders and thus are morally required to do their bidding. Well, yes and no. The manager is not morally permitted to commit illegal acts or acts that violate well-entrenched moral custom in order to increase shareholders' wealth. Moreover, we cannot assume that the stockholders necessarily want management to maximize profits. Thus, stockholders may support companies that give a certain percentage of their profits to charity. For instance, in Minnesota a number of companies give 2 percent of their profits to charity and a few give 5 percent. The fact that these companies have that policy is well known. Now individuals are free to invest their money where they choose. The stockholders in Target know, or could easily know, the company policy regarding corporate giving and invest in it nonetheless. Presumably stockholders who invest in Target do not want the policies with respect to corporate donations to change. They may not want to maximize their profits or they may think that Target's policy of corporate giving will increase customer loyalty and lead to greater profits in the long run.

This discussion is of more than theoretical interest. Social investing is a large business. People engage in social investing when they put their money in mutual funds that have ethical screens. Typically these funds will not invest in "sin" companies – companies that sell cigarettes, alcohol, or firearms. Some invest only in companies that have an exceptional record with respect to the environment. There is a multiplicity of these funds with different ethical screens. Whether these judgments about what is ethical and what is not are correct is beside the point. The real point is that investors choose to invest in firms where profit maximization is not the only or even the most important goal. As investors, they certainly have a property right to invest in these firms if they choose to. And if the agency theory is correct, managers in these businesses have an obligation to manage in accord with the principles of the firm rather than managing to maximize profits. The managers have an obligation to continue their charitable giving because presumably that is what the stockholders want.

A third problem for the orthodox view has already been mentioned. The class of stockholders is not a homogeneous set. As we noted above, one cannot assume that all stockholders want to maximize profits. Moreover, there are long-term investors and there are arbitrageurs whose time horizon is especially short. Suppose a company has both kinds of stockholders. To which group of stockholders does management have the highest obligation? As we said earlier, we see no reason why priority should go to the arbitrageur. This issue becomes especially "sticky" when we discuss management's obligations to its stockholders in a hostile takeover. A raider would say they would increase shareholder value by cutting corporate donations to charity. Perhaps so, but many of those shareholders do not want increased value at the cost of the corporation giving less to charity. We shall say more about this complex issue shortly.

There are other difficulties with the agency argument. John Boatright has put one of these difficulties most succinctly:

> That corporate mangers are not agents of the shareholders follows from the standard legal definition given by the second Restatement of Agency. Section 1 (1) which reads: "Agency is the fiduciary relation which results from the manifestation of consent by one person to another that the other shall act on his behalf and subject to his control, and consent by the other so to act." The crucial elements in this definition are (1) consent to the relationship, (2) the power to act on another's behalf, and (3) the element of control. None of these are present in the shareholder–management relation.[13]

As Boatright points out in defending his unconventional view, law determines the relation of directors and officers. There is no real opportunity on the part of those directors and officers to exercise genuine consent. They also have no power to act on behalf of the shareholders in the sense of changing the relationship of the shareholders to a third party. That is why the shareholders must vote on mergers or changing the bylaws. Managers cannot act on the shareholders' behalf. And as we have already pointed out, management is in no significant sense under the control of the stockholders. Managers are not agents in the traditional full-blown sense.

Where does this discussion leave us? Neither of the two theories can claim a clear-cut intellectual victory. Stakeholder theory has been successful in entering the lexicon of corporations to the point where many corporations indicate they are stakeholder-managed firms. Whether the reality matches the rhetoric is controversial. Nonetheless, there is unanimous agreement that at least one of the obligations and responsibilities of management is to tend to the interest of the stockholders and generally that means to tend to the profitability of the company. Most business ethicists would also agree that corporate law as currently written and interpreted gives a greater priority to the interests of the stockholder.

▲ LONG RUN/SHORT RUN AGAIN ▲

The minimal consensus above leaves us with a number of potential conflicts. Even if stockholders are genuine stakeholders and have a privileged position in law, the question of how to resolves disputes among the various stakeholders is still unclear. To favor the stockholder does not entail that in any conflict the decision should always be made on behalf of the stockholders. And it is certainly the case that we can change the law through the political process so that stockholders are given less of a favored position. Freeman and others point out that the law has changed in that way over the past half-century.

But suppose the interests of the stockholders and the other stakeholders are identical in the long run. Suppose that managers who treat their customers well and do well by their employees and show a sense of social responsibility to the community are those companies that do best for their stockholders in the long run. If that were true, it would narrow the differences between the stockholder approach and the stakeholder approach.

Are the interests of the stockholders and the other corporate stakeholders inconsistent in the long run? American managers are eager to know the answer to that question. The issue is in part empirical and in part conceptual. There are already identifiable measures for financial success and there is near unanimous consensus that financial success is equivalent to doing well by the stockholders. (That judgment is subject to further analysis, as we shall see.) We also need to know what it means for a company to be good to its other stakeholders – to its employees and the community, for example. Each year *Fortune* identifies the best companies to work for. It also periodically runs features on the best companies for women and the best companies for minorities. Also in ranking the best companies in America, social responsibility or service to the community is one of the factors. Suppose we assume that a company that is good to work for, good for women, and good for minorities is a company that is good to employees. Suppose that a company that ranks high on social responsibility is a company that is good to the community. If this analysis were correct, we would have some sense of what taking the interests of employees, stockholders, and the community amounts to. If we further assume that a company that is good to work for is a company that is good for managers to work for, then we have yet another stakeholder group covered. That leaves suppliers and customers. How can you tell when a company is good to its customers and good to its suppliers? In some industries, such as the auto industry, there are annual surveys of satisfaction. And for customers there are retention or loyalty measures. Whether these surveys and the ranking criteria that *Fortune* uses should be the criteria for treating stakeholders well is a serious conceptual issue.

But the criteria are not unreasonable, so let us take these criteria as a measure of stakeholder satisfaction. The empirical issue is the following. Are the companies that are the best to work for or that are the most socially responsible also the most successful financially? In other words, does a management that treats the stakeholders who are not stockholders well also end up treating the stockholders well? Unfortunately the answer to that question is mixed. Some of the firms that are the best to work for also achieve above average financial results, but some do not. And some companies that are very successful financially had bosses who were ranked as the hardest and worst to work for. More scientific studies come to the same conclusion.

The thesis that one must respond in the short term was also attacked in the popular business press by Porras and Collins's book, *Built to Last*. They examined several industries to see which companies were still around after a 50-year period, which had done well in financial terms and which had not. Upon examination, the argument went, the firms who took the long-run point of view and managed from more of a stakeholder perspective did best. Unfortunately, recent events have at least temporarily undercut some of the leaders. For example, Porras and Collins cited Ford's performance favorably and General Motors unfavorably. Recently Ford's stock has not performed well and Ford has had a number of stakeholder ethics issues. Ford SUVs have a tendency to roll over, and there was the dispute with Firestone about whether the blowouts on Ford vehicles were the result of poor-quality tires or the result of Ford's recommendations regarding tire pressure.

One recent study has been completed by the Great Place to Work Institute. If an investor had bought the 100 best companies to work for as reported in *Fortune* and had reinvested in the new list each year, the investor would have earned 10.6 percent annually. The

S & P 500 for the same time period had an annual return of 5.7 percent.[14]

So where are we? If the business case for stakeholder management can be made, then as a matter of practice there is little to separate management's obligations under stakeholder theory from management's obligations under stockholder theory. The data are inconclusive. We do know from the recent corporate accounting and governance scandals that some kinds of management malfeasance not only have a strong negative impact on stock price, but will also bankrupt the company, with disastrous results for all the stakeholders. We think that the business case is good enough to claim that stakeholder management will do the best for stockholders in the long run.

If stakeholder management does in fact bring stockholder results, what difference does it make which view the manager adopts? Both Friedmanites and non-Friedmanites can posit a relationship between profits and meeting stakeholder needs. What divides them is the strength of the causal arrow and a difference over which one should be the conscious model for managerial decision-making. We would argue on both prudential and moral grounds that management ought to adopt the stakeholder perspective. We begin with the moral argument. A stakeholder theorist takes the needs and interests of all the corporate stakeholders as ends. A stockholder theorist takes the interests and needs of the stakeholders as means to an end. The moral philosophy of Immanuel Kant (1724–1804) can be invoked here to show that the stakeholder theory is the one that should be adopted. Kant held that the motive for an action was the determinant of its morality. If something is done for the wrong motive, even if it leads to good results, the action is not a moral one. Many people think like Kantians here. If the public discovers that a manager has helped the community, by sponsoring a "Walk Against AIDS" for example, because it will help the bottom line, the public will dismiss the good deed as mere public relations. What the public forgets is that the manager also has an obligation to help the bottom line. As Ed Freeman would argue, there is no separation between the business function and the moral function.

Kant also argued that a moral motive was one that treated a person as an end and never merely as a means. Even treating people well while treating them merely as a means would be morally wrong. Many critics of "enlightened management techniques," such as quality circles and participative management, have been criticized because they merely use people as instruments for the attainment of more profit. Using people as instruments is wrong even if they are treated well in the process. Much more will be said about the obligations of managers to employees in chapter 3. However, Kant's philosophy provides a good moral argument for adopting the stakeholder approach. Indeed, an early article by Evan and Freeman was entitled "A Stakeholder Theory of the Modern Corporation: Kantian Capitalism."

There is also a prudential argument for a manager to adopt the stakeholder perspective. If the manager adopts the moral point of view and takes the needs and interests of all the various stakeholders as legitimate at face value, then the happy result may well be profitability. What may occur is what we have elsewhere characterized as the paradox of profits.[15] The paradox of profits comes to this: The more one consciously seeks profits, the less likely one is to obtain them. The more the management focuses on quality products, fair treatment of suppliers, just treatment of employees, a sense of corporate responsibility, and financial competence, the more likely the company is to be profitable. Our advice here may seem counter-intuitive because managers are so often exhorted to keep their eye on the bottom line. To some extent, we are arguing that management ought to keep its eyes on the interests of the stakeholders and the bottom line will more or less take care of itself. Thus, we think there are good moral reasons and good business reasons for saying that management ethics is to serve as an agent of the business stakeholders.

But what about the interests of the stockholder who is in it for the short term? The kind of arguments we made above will not apply to arbitrageurs, those who buy and sell on programs, momentum investors, and the like. For these traders policies that sacrifice the interests of other stakeholders may well drive up the stock price in the short term. For example, a company's stock almost always goes up in the short term whenever it lays off employees. In the context of the short run, employees are seen as a cost. If profits fall, then the stock price usually falls, so the manager desperately tries to cut costs. But is that really prudent and is it morally right? Should a manager focus on the short term and on stockholders who are in it for the short term, or should managers focus on the long term? We have returned to one of the questions raised earlier in this chapter.

Now some would argue that this question is nonsensical for one of two reasons. The first response is that the stock market really does build in long-term considerations. This is known as rational expectations theory. Thus, if the public believes that the Fed will lower interest rates in two months, that gets factored into the market now. And if investors really believe that taking care of stakeholders will benefit the stockholders in the long run, that also gets factored into the market now. Determining the truth of rational expectations theory would take us deep into complicated issues in the philosophy of science and the philosophy of economics. We cannot take that journey here. Certainly people do act now on what they believe the future will be. That is what momentum investment is all about. However, our beliefs about the future and even our actions on accurate beliefs are hardly rational, as psychologists have long pointed out. The thesis that the present stock price of a company is a rational assessment of the long-run future of the company seems implausible on its face. The dot.com bubble and the 5,000-point NASDAQ are testimony to that.

The second argument is that the short-term investor is a necessary provider of funds required in a capitalist market. Sacrificing the interests of the short-term investor will cause the kind of crisis known as a liquidity crisis. Investment will be inadequate. The second argument does have a certain amount of plausibility if one assumes that the only successful system of capitalism is finance-based. In other words, the funds that are needed to make companies grow and to finance new ventures must come from the private investment community. But growth can be self-financed through profits; companies can be taken private or stay private. The state can finance investment through an industrial policy or the provider of funds can be a network of partner banks as in Japan. Now all of these alternatives have disadvantages, but all have been given serious consideration in the United States – at least as a partial supplement – at times when our own system's performance was less than adequate. One such period was the early 1990s, when features of Japanese capitalism received serious attention. As the 1990s progressed, Japan plunged into recession and the United States prospered. Interestingly, there are US business firms that refuse to jump on the bandwagon and go public. Cargill and Accenture are two. A recent TV interview on CNBC with a senior partner at Accenture supplied the reason. "We do not want to be subject to the vicissitudes of Wall Street." By the way, both companies are doing fine.

Does a manager have a greater obligation to the other stakeholders, including the stockholders who are in it for the long term?

We would answer that question in the affirmative. The obligation of managers to short-term stockholders is complete transparency on the financial health of the firm. The obligations to other stakeholders are much more extensive. What justifies this conclusion? Reciprocity of commitment is one answer. The arbitrageurs and momentum investors have no commitment to the company they have temporarily invested in. Another answer is avoidance of harm. To honor the interest of the short-term investor, the manager often needs to harm other stakeholders. Take layoffs, for example. Far too many managers react to a financial setback with layoffs knowing that those layoffs will hurt the company in the long run. Why do they do it? To appease Wall Street's short-term investors. Given the lack of commitment shown by short-term investors, giving their interests priority is morally misplaced. In conclusion, the manager has a moral obligation to adopt the perspective of stakeholder management and a moral obligation to manage for the long term.

We certainly agree that it is difficult to manage for the long term, especially in an environment where success is measured quarter by quarter. We cannot prove that managing for the long run will benefit the stockholders in the long run as well as the other stakeholders, but there is a reasonable case that it will. And morality requires it. Thus, what managers need is the courage to be a leader in that regard. Ethical leadership is the focus of chapter 9. In the next three chapters, we will discuss some of the obligations that managers have to various corporate stakeholders.

▲ NOTES ▲

1. Milton Friedman, "The Social Responsibility of Business is to Increase Its Profits," *New York Times Magazine* (September 13, 1970), p. 126.
2. Theodore Levitt, "The Morality(?) of Advertising," *Harvard Business Review* (July–August 1970), pp. 84–92.
3. Albert Carr, "Is Business Bluffing Ethical?" *Harvard Business Review* (January–February 1968), pp. 145–6, 148.
4. William Evan and R. Edward Freeman, "A Stakeholder Theory of the Modern Corporation: Kantian Capitalism," in *Ethical Theory and Business*, 4th edition, ed. Tom L. Beauchamp and Norman E. Bowie (Upper Saddle River, NJ: Prentice Hall, 1993), p. 79.
5. We realize that many in finance would argue that the long term is always factored in. Anyone who watched the decline and fall of dot.com

stock prices would find the argument false on the face of it. Once you really get into the assumptions, however, there is an issue as to whether the assertion is one of empirical fact or whether it is a tautology true by the meaning of the terms. But that issue is much too complex to discuss here.

6. R. Edward Freeman, "A Stakeholder Theory of the Modern Corporation," in *Ethical Theory and Business*, 6th edition, ed. Tom L. Beauchamp and Norman E. Bowie (Upper Saddle River, NJ: Prentice Hall, 2001), p. 56.
7. Ibid., p. 59.
8. Michael C. Jensen and William H. Meckling, "Theory of the Firm: Managerial Behavior, Agency Costs, and Ownership Structure," *Journal of Financial Economics* 3 (1976), pp. 305–60.
9. See John Rawls, *A Theory of Justice* (Cambridge, MA: Harvard University Press, 1971). For Freeman's application see "A Stakeholder Theory," p. 63.
10. Ewald Kist, "Transparency in a Complex Society," McDonough School of Business, Georgetown University, 2002.
11. Quoted in James C. Collins and Jerry I. Porras, *Built to Last* (New York: Harper Business, 1994), p. 16.
12. Quoted in ibid., p. 57.
13. John R. Boatright, "Fiduciary Duties and the Shareholder Management Relation: Or, What's So Special About Shareholders?" *Business Ethics Quarterly* 4 (1994), pp. 393–407.
14. "Happy Companies Make Happy Investments," *Fortune* (May 27, 2002), p. 162.
15. Norman E. Bowie, "The Paradox of Profit," in papers on the *Ethics of Administration*, ed. N. Dale Wright (Provo, Utah: Brigham Young University Press, 1988).

chapter three

The Ethical Treatment of Employees

The unethical treatment of employees is a constant theme in the business ethics literature. Managers have been criticized because they invade the privacy of employees through the monitoring of their email, drug testing, and even gathering information about their genetic disposition to a disease. Sometimes employers dictate what can be done outside the job – no smoking, no skydiving, and no racecar driving. However, the most serious charge is that employees are fired or downsized for little or no reason. Job security, where a worker stayed with the same company for his or her entire working life, is a thing of the past. Not surprisingly, employee loyalty has diminished as a result. All this despite the fact that the organizational studies literature shows conclusively that when employees are treated well, productivity and profits increase. What is it about the contemporary US employment market that creates so many issues in business ethics? After we have identified these four major factors, we will use the philosophy of Immanuel Kant to provide reasons for stating that contemporary American management practice with respect to employees is wrong. We will then provide an alternative view of human resource practices that management should adopt and would be prudent to adopt. In other words, the recommended practices will be both ethical and profitable.

Employment at will

Most of the United States is governed by the principle of employment at will. That doctrine says that in the absence of a contract or specific legislative protection, a person may be fired for any reason – good reason, bad reason, or even no reason at all. Many employees actually sign a statement acknowledging that they are "at will" employees. It must be noted that we are not claiming that the employee has no protection against being fired. Federal statutes forbid firing someone on the basis of race, religious preference, ethnic origin, age, or disability as defined by law. These protections are not insignificant, although in some cases, as we shall see, they are of limited effectiveness. There is also a "public policy" exception to the employment at will doctrine. Employees who are fired because they refuse to break the law or who report others for breaking significant laws may have protection. However, as a practical matter courts have given a very limited range to the public policy exception. It should also be noted that employees who sue to gain their rights might find it very difficult to get a job in the industry if they lose or if they win. Suing an employer, like whistle-blowing on an employer, is not a career-enhancing move.

Employees as just one more factor of production

Economics textbooks treat employees as a factor of production along with land, machinery, and capital. If wages go up compared to the cost of machines, substitute machines for labor until the marginal cost of each is equal. Economically, there is no moral difference between a machine and a person.

Employees as a cost

Another factor leading to the unethical treatment of employees is the knee-jerk reaction on the part of managers to treat employees as simply a cost. The minute the profit picture changes, the first response is to cut costs, and one of the first places to find costs is employees. Many people who were white-collar workers or professionals, quite inappropriately, did not worry about layoffs and outsourcing to foreign countries so long as the victims were blue-collar employees or unskilled labor. But now these job losses have extended into their classes. In order to save money, foreign nationals in India and the Philippines are processing US tax returns for Ernst & Young and even analyzing CT and chest X-rays for American patients.[1]

Recently some companies such as Circuit City and Wal-Mart have carried this cost mentality to a new high (an ethical low). They simply fire people whose salary has risen beyond a certain point. With Circuit City this meant firing their most productive sales people – the people the company had honored with higher salaries, free vacations, and other perks of sales success. However, as Circuit City lost ground to Best Buy, they needed, they thought, to cut costs. (Perhaps management should ask itself why Circuit City had fallen so far behind Best Buy.) So they fired their best performers, and the numbers were not small. On February 5, 2003, Circuit City laid off 3,900 highly paid commission sales people. That figure represented 20 percent of Circuit City's sales staff. None of those fired were faulted for doing anything wrong. They were simply paid too much because they sold too much.[2]

Weak unions

Union membership in the private sector (the non-governmental sector) has fallen precipitously over the past 40 years. Unions serve as a collective power balance against an employer. Significantly, unions do not sign contracts that contain employment at will provisions. Indeed, firing someone must either be for cause or for contractually specified economic reasons. Just why unions have fallen on such hard times remains something of a mystery to one of the authors, Bowie – a former union president for the University of Delaware Association of University Professors. Unions remain strong in Europe and in some countries, such as Germany, there is union representation on the board of directors. The right to collectively bargain is on the United Nations list of the Declaration of Human Rights and is a feature of most international codes of business ethics. There is even an International Labor Organization (ILO) that sets standards for the ethical treatment of employees worldwide. As multinationals are forced to reform their labor practices or to impose reform on their supply chains in underdeveloped countries (for example, Nike), ILO standards are usually part of the industry code of conduct that is adopted. (We will have more to say about this issue when we discuss sweatshops in chapter 5.) Although union behavior is not always the paradigm of ethical conduct, it does have the power to correct, or at least mitigate, some of the ethical abuses of employers.

As a result of this analysis, we may have a better understanding of why the managerial treatment of employees is so embedded in ethical controversy. The management of employees takes place against the background of the employment at will doctrine without any counterbalance from unions. In addition, employees are seen as nothing more than factors of production, just like all other factors of production, and costly ones at that. They are not seen as persons deserving of respect or as investments necessary for the success of the firm. The treatment of employees will not improve markedly from the moral point of view until these underlying conditions change.

▲ WHY THESE PRACTICES ARE WRONG: ▲
A KANTIAN ANALYSIS

Many people would agree that the practices listed above are deplorable. Fewer would agree that the weakness of unions is a bad thing. Nonetheless, when practices are long-standing and attitudes are deeply ingrained, strong arguments are needed to change minds. We believe that the philosophy of Immanuel Kant, without the technical apparatus that surrounds it, fits well with our basic moral intuitions about the treatment of people and can be used to show exactly what is wrong with current management practice.

Kant's second formulation of the categorical imperative says, "So act that you treat humanity, whether in your own person or in that of another, always as an end and never as a means only."[3] This principle is widely referred to as Kant's respect for persons principle. Kant did not simply assert that human beings are entitled to respect; he had an elaborate argument for his claim. Human beings ought to be respected because human beings have dignity. For Kant, an object that has dignity is beyond price.

But why do they have dignity? They have dignity because human beings are capable of autonomy and thus are capable of self-governance. As autonomous beings capable of self-governance they are also responsible beings since autonomy and self-governance are the conditions for responsibility. A person who is not autonomous and who is not capable of self-governance is not responsible. That is why little children or the mentally ill are not considered responsible.

By self-governance, Kant meant that autonomous responsible beings are capable of making and following their own laws; they are not simply subject to the causal laws of nature. Anyone who recognizes that he or she is autonomous should recognize that he or she is responsible and thus that he or she is a moral being. It is the fact that a person is a moral being that enables Kant to say that persons have dignity. Kant says:

> Morality is the condition under which alone a rational being can be an
> end in himself because only through it is it possible to be a lawgiving
> member in the realm of ends. Thus morality, and humanity, insofar as
> it is capable of morality, alone have dignity.[4]

As a point of logic a person who recognizes that he or she is
responsible should ascribe dignity to anyone like him or her; that is,
one should ascribe dignity to other creatures that have the capacity
to be autonomous and responsible beings. Kant puts it this way:

> Rational nature exists as an end in itself. Man necessarily thinks of
> his own existence in this way, and thus far it is a subjective principle
> of human actions. Also every other rational being thinks of his
> existence on the same rational ground which holds also for myself;
> thus it is at the same time an objective principle from which, as a
> supreme practical ground, it must be possible to derive all laws of the
> will.[5]

Kant's argument for the necessity of including all other persons
within the scope of the respect for persons principle is based on
consistency. What we say about one case, namely ourselves, we must
say about similar cases, namely about human beings.

The implications of this argument based on consistency (a version
of the golden rule) and the dignity of human beings, are that
organizational relations ought by necessity to be moral relations
because an organization is a set of relationships among people. A
business is not and in point of logic cannot be viewed simply as a set
of economic relationships. As such, organizational relations are
subject to moral scrutiny.

We now evaluate the practices and attitudes we listed as inimical
to the ethical management of human resources practice. We begin
with employment at will. People want reasons for how others treat
them. Philosophers are committed to the giving of reasons as a
professional requirement. Employment at will allows a manager to
fire a person without giving a reason. The firing of a person for no
reason violates a fundamental principle of the moral life, as does
firing someone for a bad reason. Part of what it means to respect a
person is to give good reasons for actions that affect them, especially
when vital interests are at stake. People have an interest in developing certain long-range goals that ideally integrate the various parts of
their lives. Philosophers refer to this as developing a rational life
plan. Capricious treatment not based on reasons makes it impossible

to develop a rational life plan and thus capricious treatment violates the respect for persons principle. Morality requires that actions be justified and that the reasons for action be good reasons. Firing a person for no reason or a bad reason violates the canons of ethics. The employment at will doctrine is a perfect example of showing that what is legal is not necessarily moral.

We now turn to the attitudes that govern treating employees as factors of production. That persons have a dignity that the other factors of production do not have requires that employees be treated with respect. As we have shown, persons are entitled to respect because they are free, rational, moral beings capable of being held responsible. No other factor of production is like that. Thus on moral grounds, machines cannot be simply substituted for employees if that would deny treating them with respect. Firing them whenever the cost of employees rises compared to another factor of production does not treat them with respect.

Some might argue that when employees accept a job they recognize and thus freely accept an employment condition where they know that machines might replace them if it is technologically possible to do so and the marginal cost of employees exceeds the marginal cost of the machines. If that were true, firing them would be consistent with respect for persons, because the autonomy of employees was respected during the hiring process.

When unemployment is low, there might be some merit to this argument, although even here the acceptance is probably more implicit than explicit. But when unemployment is relatively high, then the argument is more problematic. For much of their lives people need to work to eat. When unemployment is high, they must take any job they can get – even when the conditions of employment are highly undesirable. Acceptance in this type of situation does not seem like acceptance in any real sense.

This moral argument is reinforced when we consider the practice of looking at employees simply as costs. Our claim here is that looking at employees simply as costs is both prudentially and ethically stupid. First, an employee is a person and is thus more than a cost. To treat a person simply as a cost is to violate Kant's respect for persons principle. In addition, an employee is an investment. Firing an employee who has just received thousands of dollars' worth of training is not an action that should be taken lightly. Several studies have documented the costs of the premature firing of employees who need to be replaced with novices, who in turn need training when the economy turns around. Frederick Reichheld has documented the gains in employee loyalty and the savings in training that result from a policy that does not lay off workers whenever there is a negative blip in the profit picture. Attempts to find alternatives to layoffs, especially when the negative financial picture seems temporary and not too severe, are ethically and prudentially superior to much current practice.

The behavior of Circuit City and Wal-Mart described above is especially unsettling. These firms not only violate the respect for persons principle, but they violate a principle of just deserts as well. Both corporations argue that salaries are commensurate with productivity. In other words, they have been earned. The actions of Circuit City turn this fundamental principle of justice on its head. In addition, such action seems dumb from a business sense. It is like a farmer selling off his most productive stud stock simply because they are more expensive to maintain.

There is no Kantian argument that requires that a society support unionization. However, once we turn to the implementation of the respect for persons principle, we can see why unionization would be supported. How can the autonomy of a worker be protected? Unionization has seemed such a natural answer that it is now considered a universal right. In addition, every major international code of business ethics, such as the United Nations Global Compact and the Caux Roundtable Principles for Business, endorses a right to unionization. The United States is one of the least supportive of unionization in the highly industrialized countries. We are not living up to the higher ethical standards of Europe and Japan with respect to our treatment of employees. European companies see unions in a far less adversarial way than American managers. In some European countries and in a few American companies, unions have representation on the board. American companies should adopt as a matter of policy what some American unions have negotiated as a matter of contract: management neutrality. Management neutrality occurs when managers pledge not to actively oppose a union organization drive in a non-union plant or facility – as might happen in a merger or acquisition, for example. On a more positive note, Ford has negotiated an agreement with its unions, that it would "encourage" its suppliers not to oppose unionization.[6]

▲ THE ETHICAL TREATMENT OF EMPLOYEES ▲
IN THE MORAL FIRM

As a first step in treating employees ethically, companies should reject the employment at will doctrine. It should be pointed out that Europe rejects employment at will as do most highly developed nations. The United States is out of step with the rest of the world on this issue and it is morally wrong. Some states have shown some interest in constraining employment at will. Maine came within one vote of such restraints in the 2002–3 session. In addition, the labor laws of the 1930s should be strengthened so that it is more difficult to fire workers who support a union. In theory that is illegal now, but the reality is quite different.

In addition to these macro changes that are primarily changes in public policy, we need to determine the specific obligations of managers in this area. In other words, let us adopt a more positive and idealistic approach and ask what a firm where employees were treated well would look like. What are the moral obligations of managers to employees? We shall argue that managers are obligated to give employees a reasonable wage, reasonable benefits, job security, a voice regarding working conditions, and meaningful work. We group the first three items under the generic term "economic benefits."

▲ ECONOMIC BENEFITS ▲

There is little doubt that people want a certain amount of economic security with their job. Ideally, this would include a reasonable salary, a standard benefit package, and job security. Of course people want that, but is there any moral obligation to provide it, and even if there were such a moral obligation, could business fulfill it? After all, economists would argue that economic benefits are determined by a competitive marketplace and not by moral philosophy. And to a large extent that is certainly true, but the issues are more complicated than that.

First, the moral obligation has to be suitably qualified. Wages must be considered in context. There are jobs that introduce young people to the world of work or that supplement retirement and social security income. McDonald's is a classic example of such an employer. Also, low pay may not be a moral issue with a sufficiently high negative income tax (workers with very low incomes now receive checks from the government rather than pay income tax on the meager salaries they earn). It is estimated that 40 million American workers pay no income tax. Also, low pay is less of an issue if adequate health insurance is available. Unfortunately, low-paying jobs and jobs without health insurance tend to go together.

Market considerations do impact the ability of firms to provide retirement benefits and health insurance. That is why most industrialized countries have a national health insurance plan. Health care costs have outpaced inflation for much of the last 50 years, roughly the time when health insurance became a more or less standard benefit. Perhaps the obligation to provide health care or health insurance falls on government rather than business.

As for job security, total job security is impossible in the highly competitive world of international business competition. Moreover, technology sometimes makes a product obsolete. Perhaps in today's world what is needed is a longer period to collect unemployment insurance and more training for employees.

These remarks seem to indicate that business has a very limited, if any, moral obligation with respect to wages, benefits, and job security. If any institution has an obligation in these areas, it is government and not business. We agree that government does have a considerable obligation here and that government has not lived up to its obligations. Before letting business off the hook entirely, a few considerations need to be addressed.

The claim that business normally owed employees a fair wage, benefits, and job security was accepted by business for many years. Indeed, in human-resource circles, reference was made to the social contract with business. In return for a fair wage, benefits, and job security, an employee was obligated to provide a honest day's work for a honest day's pay, and to be loyal to the employer. Employees ought not simply to have taken a slightly higher-paying position, if the employer was keeping up his end of the social contract.

Employers argue that the old social contract is outdated and impractical, and that employees must realize that there is a new social contract with employees. However, as Pfeffer has pointed out, this new social contract is hardly a contract in any meaningful sense since it was imposed on employees.[7] It is also morally deficient because there is no benefit to the employee from the new social contract. A contract freely entered into is supposed to benefit both sides. How does a loss of benefits and job security with no offsetting rise in salary benefit employees? The so-called "new social contract" is unethical on its face, and for management to impose such a contract on employees is unethical.

Nonetheless, it is possible that the old social contract is less practical today than it was in 1950. Perhaps it needs to be changed. However, business is morally obligated to make the case. Perhaps the realities of international competition do require changes. However, managers are obligated to discuss these changes with employees, to be fully transparent about the competitive situation they face, and to provide substitute benefits for the ones that are lost. For example, if job security is to become more problematic, then managers are obligated to provide more training so that employees are employable elsewhere. If more workers were unionized, then such issues would be negotiated. In the absence of unionization and with wages, benefits, and job security under competitive pressure, the obligation of managers to provide participation and a voice is even stronger.

Finally, managers cannot claim that the government must take more responsibility for unemployment insurance, health insurance, and other traditional benefits that were assumed to be the responsibility of business while at the same time lobbying against every attempt by government to find tax revenues to support such programs. To argue that government should provide these benefits and then lobby against government provision of them is the height of hypocrisy. Neither can they move their headquarters offshore to avoid taxes, nor can they set up elaborate schemes for the avoidance of state taxes as WorldCom and KPMG did.[8] In light of the insistence that companies must abandon the traditional social contract, these activities are morally wrong.

▲ PARTICIPATION AND VOICE ▲

As we have seen, for a Kantian, freedom or autonomy is the central value and the ground of ethics. Of course a Kantian does not endorse the freedom to deny freedom to others. Political philosophers have put the freedom principle this way: Everyone should be permitted as much freedom as possible compatible with a like freedom for all. In what follows "freedom" will be used in this sense. Organizational structures and activities that support freedom are good and those that inhibit freedom are bad. Thus, managers should try to manage so that workers are given as much freedom as possible consistent with the goals of providing goods and services at a profit. A management ethics committed to this goal of enhancing freedom would institute revolutionary changes in American business.

A major inhibitor of worker freedom is the existence of the hierarchical organization. The traditional organization chart shows who reports to whom; persons higher in the organization chart give orders to those lower in the organization and these persons are supposed to comply. Some economists, such as Oliver Williamson, believe that this is the only truly efficient way to organize a firm.[9] If employees' freedom is reduced, that is the price to be paid by an efficient organization. If these economists are right, then we have an ethical dilemma: increased freedom or increased efficiency.

Perhaps this is a false dilemma, as recent evidence has shown the efficacy of alternative organization forms. There is a greater use of teamwork, especially where quality is concerned. Indeed, where improved quality is the chief goal, these teams are often called quality circles. Teams make decisions collectively. The range of collective responsibility given to teams varies widely from company to company, but in some cases it is truly extensive. What to order, whom to hire, whom to discipline, changes in procedure can all be decided by the team rather than by a supervisor.

Ironically, a phenomenon that we have criticized on ethical grounds – downsizing – can be supportive of increased autonomy. By eliminating layers of management and making a flatter organization, employees have fewer supervisors and less supervision, They are also likely to have more responsibility. They are also expected to be more creative and innovative. The organizational structure becomes less hierarchical and more team or task oriented. All this represents gains in autonomy but at the price of less job security.

Another inhibitor of workers' freedom is the existence of high information asymmetry. One example of high information asymmetry occurs when managers have information that other workers do not. The success of teams and less adversarial relations with unions requires less information asymmetry. One management technique for reducing information asymmetry is open-book management. Under open-book management, all employees have access to all the financial information in the firm. As the founder of open-book management, Jack Stack, put it, the goal of open-book management is to make everyone in the firm – even the person who pushes the broom – a kind of chief financial officer. Increasing the amount of information available enhances participation and hence autonomy. Studies of open-book management show that it contributes mightily to the bottom line and is consistent with Kantian respect for persons. In a video describing Springfield Remanufacturing Company as a winner of a business ethics award, an employee says of open-book management, "It makes me feel like a person."

▲ MEANINGFUL WORK ▲

In addition to good pay, benefits, job security, participation and voice, managers also have an obligation to try to provide meaningful work. We admit at the outset that "meaningful work" is a contested concept. However, we shall define meaningful work from the Kantian perspective of this chapter. For a Kantian, the following characteristics would be definitive of meaningful work:

1. Meaningful work is work that is freely entered into.
2. Meaningful work allows the worker to exercise his or her autonomy and independence.
3. Meaningful work enables the worker to develop his or her rational capacities.
4. Meaningful work provides a wage sufficient for physical welfare.
5. Meaningful work supports the moral development of employees.
6. Meaningful work is not paternalistic in the sense of interfering with the worker's conception of how he or she wishes to obtain happiness.[10]

It should be noted that a large part of this definition of meaningful work has already been discussed under economic benefits, participation, and voice. Characteristic 6 deserves special comment, however. Some companies try to get employees to adopt a certain lifestyle – to avoid dangerous activities, to stop smoking, to avoid getting too fat. This is to try to impose one view of what is best for one on another. A Kantian rejects this kind of paternalism. Perhaps a company can point out the health risks associated with certain activities but that should be the end of the matter. Education is morally permissible. Forbidding certain activities is not.

Kant's emphasis on avoiding paternalism can be linked to contemporary language regarding an employee's right to privacy.
Privacy rights advocates object to a company forbidding extreme
sports, smoking, drinking, and the like on grounds that monitoring
such activities would be a violation of an employee's right to privacy.
Privacy rights advocates also object to the electronic monitoring of
employees, genetic testing to determine whether an employee has a
predisposition to a disease, and prohibitions on dating between
employees. Most employees claim a moral right to privacy and they
sometimes have a legal right as well. It should be noted, however,
that the Bill of Rights of the US Constitution does not apply to the
corporation. There is no right to free speech in the corporation. If a
provision of the Constitution does apply, it is only through further
federal or state legislative enactment.

What normative grounds can be given for these rights? The most
effective ground is a Kantian one. The best formulation of the
Kantian argument is by Joseph Kupfer, who grounds the argument
in the Kantian idea of autonomy and respect for persons.[11] Kupfer
starts with the assumption that autonomy is a basic value. He then
sets out to show that the development of a self-concept is a necessary
condition for the development of autonomy and that in turn privacy
is a necessary condition for the development of a self-concept.
Kupfer cites a number of studies to show that privacy is necessary
for a sense of control over one's life, which is necessary for the
development of autonomy. People in controlled environments like
prisons, hospitals, and military establishments can lose this sense of
control and have their development as autonomous beings delayed
or even reversed. He also argues that we need privacy to test out
options in a possible life plan without running real-life risks. We
need privacy to show we are trustworthy, and privacy is necessary
for the intimacy that enables us to develop relationships in different
ways. We have an intimacy with friends and lovers that distinguishes
them from co-workers and acquaintances. The ability to choose the
quality of our relationships with people, the ability to be trusted and
trustworthy, and the ability to develop goals, purposes, or even a
plan for one's life are all necessary for the development of
autonomous selves, and privacy is a necessary condition of them all.

Even if privacy rights are well grounded, there are still issues
concerning when such rights may be overruled by other ethical
considerations. For example, many have objected to the drug testing
of employees on privacy grounds. However, employees on drugs

present a danger to other corporate stakeholders – to other employees and customers. There is now a consensus in the United States that protecting other stakeholders from harm justifies overriding any privacy claims with respect to drug testing. Drug testing of employees is now standard practice.

To do justice to each of the privacy claims that have been made on behalf of employees is beyond the scope of this book. The general points are valid, however. Managers should recognize that employees have a right to privacy. This privacy right should only be overridden to protect another right of a corporate stakeholder. Violation of the right merely to save money is not sufficient moral grounds for the rights violation. What is disturbing to us is how often privacy rights are ignored simply on the grounds that a company can save money. Each case, however, must be considered in context.

We shall provide one example of how a company might reason about two cases and come to different conclusions about a manager's obligations to respect privacy. We think different conclusions are morally appropriate when a business considers the genetic testing of employees and when they charge smokers more than non-smokers for health insurance. Genetic testing is done to determine whether a person has a predisposition to a disease. Suppose that a business, on discovering that such a predisposition exists, fires the employee because if he or she contracts the disease, the company's health insurance costs would go up. This would be an unethical invasion of privacy. The person is not responsible for their genes. The connection between the disposition to the disease and actually getting the disease is probabilistic and, in most cases, many people who have the disposition do not get the disease. Also, it is unjust to penalize someone for something over which they have no control. In the case of smokers, there is a well-known link between acts of smoking and disease, and an employee is arguably responsible for his or her smoking in a way that he or she is not responsible for his or her genes. Thus, non-smoking employees have a justice argument that they should not support the harmful behavior of smokers. Note, however, that we do not permit firing smokers or refusing to hire them, although we do support a non-smoking policy in the workplace and charging them more – even considerably more – for their health insurance premiums. This example is designed to provide some insight into how a manager should reason about such issues when privacy rights are at stake.

It should be noted that five of the six characteristics are all justified on the grounds of a Kantian theory of human nature with its emphasis on rational autonomy. The argument for a reasonable wage is derived from Kant's imperfect duty of beneficence when applied to organizations. Kant distinguished between perfect duties and imperfect duties. Perfect duties are duties that are always in force (do not lie) and imperfect duties are duties that must be honored on occasion but are not always in force (aid those in need.) Kant's argument for this duty of beneficence was based on the fact that no rational person would have others deny aid if he or she were in need, therefore he or she has a duty to aid others. A similar argument could be used to show that the business equivalent of a duty of beneficence is the duty to pay a reasonable wage.

This conversation is still fairly abstract. Let us show how these six principles can be implemented in a business context. Let us begin with the issue of a reasonable wage. Even if the market predominantly determines wages, there are some things management can do to make its compensation scheme more just and more easily conformable to the requirement that managers pay a reasonable wage. Wage compression refers to a policy that reduces large differences in pay between the top officials in the corporation and other employees. Note that wage compression would attack the growing gap between executive compensation and compensation of the average worker. It also refers to a policy that reduces differences between employees at the same functional level. If wage compression were adopted horizontally, the Vice-President for Finance would not earn a premium over the Vice-President for Personnel, as is now the case in most US corporations. Most important, wage compression would address one of the causes of having work and being poor.

One key is employer-sponsored training. This becomes especially crucial if the old social contract really is not viable. Training increases the skills one has and that in turn opens up new opportunities – both for work in the company that provides the training and more potential future work in other companies should the employee's own company engage in downsizing. Cross-utilization and cross-training is a technique that allows employees to do many different jobs. This kind of training is a specific way of training that allows workers to perform a number of tasks. It is an excellent way to overcome the limitations of specialization as seen in Adam Smith's pin factory. Overspecialization leads to boredom whereas cross-training and cross-utilization enables workers to take a more holistic approach to the work and to avoid boredom. This kind of training enhances autonomy because it gives the worker more opportunities, increases the number of skills the worker has, and allows the worker a wider range of experiences. This kind of training has been a feature of Japanese management, which has been adopted by progressive managers in the United States.

Another key is to eliminate policies and practices that create class differences among people that undermine self-respect. Symbolic egalitarianism refers to the elimination of such status symbols. Status symbols undermine the self-esteem of the persons who do not have symbols. Where these symbols can easily be eliminated, respect for persons requires that they should be. For example, why should managers have parking spots closer to the door? Is the principle of first come first served not the just principle? And why should we have executive dining rooms? They are both expensive and needlessly disrespectful of non-executives.

Companies should adopt the system of open-book management mentioned earlier. We have already pointed out that information asymmetry provides many opportunities for unethical behavior. The opposite, information sharing, is just the opposite because it provides opportunities for the greater exercise of one's autonomy. The greater the knowledge you have, the larger the number of your options and possibilities for choice. Information sharing reaches an apex when all the financial information regarding the firm is shared with all employees.

In addition to greater sharing of information, decision-making in teams increases empowerment. With some teams, the team hires and fires. Choosing with whom one will work can be extremely em-powering. Instead of taking all one's orders from a boss, team decision-making gives the employee more control over his or her work life.

In this section of the chapter we have tried to provide some organizational alternatives to the way human resources are typically managed. Our main concern is that human resource management is practiced in an ethical manner. Kant's respect for persons principle serves as the moral foundation for ethical human resource manage-ment. However, we are acutely aware that a business needs to make a profit. And we also are acutely aware of the "ought implies can" rule. A necessary condition for one to have a moral obligation to do something is that the person can in fact do it. As we said initially, we believe that the ethical form of human resource management espoused here is not only compatible with profit but also that it enhances long-run profit. A minority of executives accepts a view of human resource management not dissimilar to our own. Max DePree, former CEO of Miller Furniture, captured the Kantian ideal when he described work as follows:

> For many of us who work there exists an exasperating discontinuity between how we see ourselves as persons and how we see ourselves as workers. We need to eliminate the sense of discontinuity and to restore a sense of coherence in our lives Work can be and should be productive and rewarding, meaningful and maturing, enriching and fulfilling, healing and joyful. Work is one of the great privileges. Work can even be poetic.
>
> What is it most of us really want from work? We would like to find the most effective, most productive, most rewarding way of working together. We would like to know that our work process uses all of the appropriate and pertinent resources: human, physical, and financial. We would like a work process and relationships that meet our personal needs for belonging, for contributing, for meaningful work, for the opportunity to make a commitment, for the opportunity to grow and be at least reasonably in control of our own destinies.[12]

▲ THE BUSINESS CASE FOR THE ETHICAL ▲ TREATMENT OF EMPLOYEES – THE TEST CASE OF LAYOFFS

The obligation that managers provide job security is the human resource obligation on our list most likely to be ridiculed. In today's world, job security is an impossibility, they would argue, but the evidence cuts the other way as layoffs are not a guarantee of greater profits. A study cited in the *Wall Street Journal* shows that after two years, the stock prices of two thirds of the companies who downsized lagged behind the stock prices of comparable firms by 5 percent to 45 percent. In addition, the stock prices of 50 percent of the companies who downsized lagged behind the general market by 17 percent to 48 percent.[13] Overall productivity can also be hurt by layoffs. Pfeffer cites a study that shows that for 1977–87, a third of those companies that downsized experienced significant correlative decreases in productivity. At the same time, of those companies who increased employment, 52 percent experienced significant increases in productivity.[14]

In addition, layoffs in an economic downturn add costs later. If possible, the rational manager should try not to lay off her employees in such a situation. Why? When firms lay off people, the labor pool usually increases and the cost of labor falls in accordance with the laws of supply and demand. When conditions improve, they often improve for most firms simultaneously. This draws down the supply of labor and, as a result, the cost of labor increases. Firms that engaged in the most extensive layoffs will have to replace labor at a higher cost and, of course, incur the cost of retraining. Although it is hard to quantify these factors, it is likely that these costs in conjunction with the loss in productivity, conjoined with such intangibles as costs to loyalty and morale, call into question the strategy behind many layoffs. Such firms would be better served by taking into account the cyclical pattern of their hiring needs and trying to avoid layoffs if they can. Indeed, in the right individual circumstances, a firm should try to hire additional employees when other firms are laying them off.

Moreover, it can even be expensive to hire back the same employees – if you can. Often during a layoff, the severance agreement stipulates that the employee cannot return to the firm. They could not be hired back even if managers wanted to. According to an American Management Association survey of 720 companies, 30 percent of companies that downsized brought back the laid-off employees either by rehiring them outright or engaging them for consulting services. Of course it is natural to think that hiring them as consultants is cheaper, but often it is not, as in the advertising industry, for example.[15]

If this no layoff strategy still sounds too utopian, consider the behavior of Southwest Airlines. After the terrorist attacks on the United States on September 11, 2001, every airline except Southwest believed that they had to cut service and lay off employees. Southwest maintained its schedule and laid no one off. It continued to prosper and take market share from its competitors. The low-cost arm of US Airways went out of business. At the Baltimore Washington International (BWI) Airport, US Airways had long been dominant. Today US Airways has several gates in one terminal but Southwest Airlines now has gates in one full terminal and part of another. Southwest is now the dominant airline at BWI.

Additional evidence of the costs of downsizing comes from the work of Frederick Reichheld. Among the important evidence he cites in his book *The Loyalty Effect* are an American Management

Association study and a *Wall Street Journal* study. The former shows that after five years, less than half the companies that have downsized have increased their profits and that only a third have increased their productivity. The latter study indicated that after three years of restructuring, the restructured suffered a negative 24 percent growth rate compared to the Standard & Poor's 500. In other studies, Reichheld is able to show a high inverse correlation between employee turnover and productivity. When one chain ranked its stores, "it found that the top third in employee retention was also the top third in productivity with a 22% higher sales per employee than the bottom third." The most profitable of the national brokerage houses, A. G. Edwards, also had the highest retention rate. Reichheld reported that the total cost of hiring a new broker was $100,000. New brokers will not earn any profit for their firm until the third year. More than half the new brokers will not last more than three years, which pushes the real investment to $300,000 per broker. What does that mean in terms of broker retention? An increase in broker retention from 80 percent to 90 percent will increase the value of a new broker by 155 percent.[16]

Apple Computer serves as a poignant example of the irreparable harm that can be caused by layoffs. In its early days, under the leadership of Steve Jobs and Stephen Wozniak, Apple produced what many considered the best technology in computers. At the same time, Apple exhibited a unique culture that boasted high employee morale. Here is one case where a corporate handbook celebrating the importance of people to firms' success was actually consistent with actual practice. Apple was known for employee accessibility to management, recognition of employee milestones, and bagels and cream cheese on Fridays. The devotion of employees was even considered "cult-like."

But Apple was locked in a tough competitive struggle with Microsoft. When John Scully replaced Steve Jobs, a new management style was adopted. Unlike Jobs, Scully subscribed to the traditional management philosophy. He saw employees as costs and believed that to compete successfully with Microsoft, some of these labor costs had to be eliminated. Apple began a series of layoffs in 1985 followed by more rounds in 1991. Eventually 10 percent of the labor force was cut. But things did not improve and Scully was fired; the layoff policy continued under Scully's successor. Fourteen percent of the Apple workforce was laid off in 1993 and yet another layoff occurred in 1997. At that point, Apple had less than half of its original workforce, and for the remaining workers there were no more bagels and cream cheese. You can quantify the costs of bagels and cream cheese, but what the cost-cutters forget is that you cannot quantify the benefits of having people get together to discuss and resolve issues. Despite the cost-cutting, Apple's downward spiral continued. Finally Steve Jobs was persuaded to return and lead the company. He got rid of the cost-cutting penalty and focused on new and better products. The Apple iMac is considered a leader in its field. Recently Apple introduced software (iTunes) to allow the downloading of music while sufficiently protecting the intellectual property of the recording industry. Microsoft is still a formidable competitor and the future success of Apple is far from guaranteed. However, the introduction of new products and superior technology seems more effective as a competitive strategy than does aggressive cost-cutting. We are not so naïve as to believe that layoffs are never necessary, but they should be the last resort, not the first resort. Across the board salary cuts and reduced hours for all employees might be viable alternatives. In any case, it is well to remember that there is a lot of evidence to show that frequent downsizing does *not*, contrary to the conventional wisdom, bring about rightsizing.

▲ CONCLUSION ▲

In this chapter we have focused on the ethical practice of human resource management. We have provided some general goals for ethical human resource management: a reasonable wage, good benefits, job security, a voice in management decision-making, and meaningful work. We have also provided some specific ideas on how these goals could be achieved – teams and quality circles, open-book management, a commitment to compress the wage gap between senior managers and the rank and file. Finally, we have tried to show how these goals and the means to implement them are not simply the ideals of impractical philosophers, but are grounded in the business reality that a business needs to make money to stay in business.

▲ NOTES ▲

1. Nelson D. Schwartz, "Down and Out in White Collar America," *Fortune* (June 23, 2003), p. 80. The issue of outsourcing American jobs

has become a major political issue as well. As this manuscript was in final preparation *Business Week* had a featured commentary "Outsourcing Jobs: Is It Bad?" (August 18–25, 2003).

2. All references to the Circuit City case are from Carlos Tejada and Gary McWilliams, "New Recipe for Cost Savings: Replace Expensive Workers," *Wall Street Journal* (June 11, 2003), pp. A1, A12.

3. This section is taken directly from Norman Bowie's book, *Business Ethics: A Kantian Perspective* (Malden, MA: Blackwell, 1999). The quotation is from Immanuel Kant, *Foundations of the Metaphysics of Morals* [1785], trans. L. W. Beck (New York: Macmillan, 1990), p. 46.

4. Kant, *Foundations*, p. 52.

5. Ibid., p. 36.

6. Bill Vlasic, "Why Ford is Riding Shotgun for the UAW," *Business Week* (March 17, 1997), p. 112.

7. Jeffrey Pfeffer, *The Human Equation* (Boston: Harvard Business School Press, 1996), chapter 6.

8. The details of this morally outrageous behavior can be found in "WorldCom Tax Strategy May Have Helped It Save Millions," *Wall Street Journal* (August 13, 2003), pp. C1, C9.

9. Oliver E. Williamson, *Markets and Hierarchies* (New York: Free Press, 1975).

10. This list is taken from Norman Bowie "A Kantian Theory of Meaningful Work," *Journal of Business Ethics* 17 (1998), pp. 1083–92, and Bowie, *Business Ethics: A Kantian Perspective*.

11. Joseph Kupfer, "Privacy, Autonomy, and Self-Concept," *American Philosophical Quarterly* 24 (January, 1987), pp. 81–7.

12. Max DePress, *Leadership is an Art* (Dell Publishing, 1989), pp. 23, 32.

13. J. R. Dorfman, "Stocks of Companies Announcing Layoffs Fire Up Investors, But Profits Often Wilt," *Wall Street Journal* (December 10, 1991), pp. C1, C2.

14. Pfeffer, *The Human Equation*, p. 174.

15. Ibid.

16. These studies are cited in Frederick F. Reichheld, *The Loyalty Effect* (Boston: Harvard Business School Press, 1996).

The Ethical Treatment of Customers

It is not a stretch to say that the most crucial stakeholder in any business is its customers. Without customers, there would be no business and no profits for stockholders. This is so obvious, yet many firms have run into difficulty when they forgot their customers. It is interesting to note that some of the better-known examples of business ethics are about firms that have explicitly put their customers first, and many of the infamously bad examples of business ethics represent firms that have harmed their customers. Ford Motor Company had the Pinto and then the Explorer SUV with the Firestone tires. Sears Auto Repair shops in California did repairs that were not needed. Beechnut Nutrition Company sold apple juice for babies that it had reason to believe was adulterated. When these dangers and deceptions were discovered these companies paid handsomely in the marketplace and/or in the court system.

On the other hand, when several people died from poison that had been put in capsules of Tylenol, Johnson & Johnson used its credo to take action that although costly in the short run saved the brand and earned them a place in the lexicon of business ethics heroes. The Johnson & Johnson credo begins as follows:

> We believe our first responsibility is to the doctors, nurses and patients, to mothers and fathers and all others who use our products and services. In meeting their needs everything we do must be of high quality. We must constantly strive to reduce our costs in order to maintain reasonable prices. Customers' orders must be serviced promptly and accurately.

The CEO at the time of the Tylenol poisonings, James Burke, indicated that the decision to recall the product was an easy one given the company's credo. The *first* responsibility of Johnson &

Johnson was to the patients. Later, when additional poisonings occurred, Johnson & Johnson made the decision to abandon capsules and to replace them with caplets. Both decisions were expensive and risky. Even the government had not recommended a product recall and the FBI apparently had actually discouraged it. Tylenol regained its market share and Johnson & Johnson remains synonymous with good business ethics in the minds of consumers.

In this chapter we will consider the ethical obligations of managers to customers. An important concept underlies most of our discussion. Many of the ethical issues surrounding the treatment of customers can be understood as issues of information asymmetry. The seller usually has information that the buyer does not know and could not be reasonably expected to know. In chapter 1 we defined information asymmetry as a situation where one person or persons in a relationship had knowledge that other persons in the relationship did not have and to which the other persons had a legal or moral right. Information asymmetry is abused when the person with the information withholds it from those who have a legal or moral right to it. The major issue up for discussion is: What information do customers have a moral right to have? Only when we know the answer to that question can we determine whether a customer was deceived in a purchase or just behaved foolishly and should have known better.

▲ WHAT DOES A CUSTOMER HAVE ▲ A RIGHT TO KNOW?

This issue has not escaped the analysis of business ethicists. David Holley has identified five rules that might serve as standards a sales manager might follow.[1] Holley correctly rejects the two extremes – what he calls the minimal information rule and the maximal information rule. The minimal rule places the whole burden on the consumer; the salesperson has no obligation to provide information the consumer does not ask for. The maximal rule places way too much responsibility on the seller since it would require the salesperson to have a positive obligation to inform the consumer of any information that would be relevant in making the purchase. No responsibility is placed on the consumer. Under the maximal rule, for example, a salesperson would be obligated to tell the customer that a sale was in progress across the street and that the consumer could get this product cheaper from the competitor. In reality both the consumer and the seller have some responsibility for obtaining information. We believe that price comparison in most situations is the responsibility of the consumer. On the other hand, in most cases the salesperson has some obligation to the customer. Most products are not like cantaloupes on display in the supermarket. The quality of the cantaloupes can be determined by the customer. Most of the products we buy have no relation to cantaloupes; they are highly sophisticated and technical. Their quality is not easily open to inspection and the consumer is dependent on the salesperson for important information. Certainly information that is relevant to the safe use of the product is required. Holley refers to this rule as the modified minimal information rule. That is why the government requires that side effects be mentioned in pharmaceutical ads and why a list of ingredients is a part of food labeling. Someone who is allergic to peanuts needs to know if there is any peanut product in what he or she is buying. His or her life may depend on it. Holley is right to insist that the seller is obligated to provide information to the buyer that will enable him to avoid risk of injury. However, Holley believes that the modified minimal information rule is insufficient. He believes that salespersons are required to provide information that goes beyond safety information. Holley's most plausible candidates for an adequate criterion are the fairness rule and the mutual benefit rule. The fairness rule divides the responsibility between the seller and the customer by requiring the salesperson to provide information needed to make a reasonable judgment about whether to purchase a product that the buyer could not be expected to know without the information from the seller. The mutual benefit rule requires much more of the seller since it requires that the salesperson provide any information needed to make a reasonable judgment about whether to purchase a product that the buyer does not possess. In the fairness rule the key terms are "what the buyer could not be expected to know," while in the mutual benefit rule the key terms are "that the buyer does not possess." The crucial issue here morally is whether the buyer has the responsibility to possess the information. Did the buyer undertake the search costs that would be expected of a reasonable consumer? Holley believes that if the fairness rule is adopted, the vulnerable consumer will not be protected. Holley is rightly concerned about the information that the elderly, the mentally impaired, and the uneducated do not receive. We agree that there should be more stringent rules in selling to vulnerable populations and we will turn to this issue shortly.

▲ OBLIGATIONS TO THE RATIONAL ▲ CONSUMER

For the moment, let us focus on the mythical rational consumer. We agree that the fairness rule is roughly right. However, there are some clarifications and caveats that need to be addressed. Although the "rational person" standard is common in law, in the "real" world there is considerable disagreement over who should count as a rational person. We do not think there is a fixed definition, but a high-school diploma should be sufficient, as should the ability to live on one's own without state assistance.

What should be noted is that even if most of us should undertake considerable search costs so that we have the information a reasonable person would want to know in purchasing a product, many current sales practices would not meet this criterion. There is a simple reason for this. Too often salespeople and the incentive structures in the companies that support them are geared to maximizing the value of a sale. That is, the goal is to sell the highest priced item possible even if the salesperson knows that the highest priced model is not what the person needs. Suppose the criterion for the obligation of salespersons was to try to determine the true needs of the customer and then sell them the product that most fits their need. In so doing, the salesperson hopes that the customer will become a repeat customer on the basis of that behavior. If a person wants a stereo system for their apartment, do not sell him or her one for a large home. Sell the customer a smaller one for the apartment and have them come back when they buy the larger home. That is the stance that the ethical sales manager ought to adopt and the philosophy that should be instilled in the sales force.

Of course, if the emphasis is on a quick sale and a one-time transaction, many salespeople will not follow the moral rule. However, we maintain that it is the obligation of a sales manager to create an incentive system for salespeople in the organization to meet the needs of the consumer with an eye to repeat business. An ethical manager makes a profit by meeting consumer needs. An unethical manager makes a profit by exploiting information asymmetry and having the sales staff maximize the selling price, regardless of consumer need. Changing prevalent sales practice is an issue of management ethics because only managers can revise the incentive systems that support present sales practice.

▲ ISSUES OF FAIRNESS ▲

In addition to information asymmetry as an organizing concept for thinking about a manager's obligations to customers, fairness represents the other major organizing concept. Of course, "fairness" means different things to different people. A common thread, however, seems to be that managers should not take advantage of situations over which the consumer has no control. The economic laws of supply and demand indicate that merchants should raise prices when demand picks up and often that is true – but not always. People consider merchants who raise the price of snow shovels after a blizzard or the price of candles after a hurricane are engaging in unfair pricing – no matter what the laws of economics say. And if the price rises are significant enough, pricing that is unfair becomes illegal and goes under the term "price gouging." If pricing is simply a matter of supply and demand, why are there laws against price gouging?

Sales managers may argue that the views of customers regarding fairness are not consistent. Psychologists have shown that people have dispositions to respond favorably to discounts but will not accept increases. For example, they will accept the fairness of an early bird special at a restaurant, but they will think a surcharge for diners at peak times to be unfair. Thus, restaurants are ill-advised to raise prices to patrons if they arrive after six. But early bird specials are OK. Suppose you like to dine at seven. People are outraged if a restaurant raises the price of a steak from $12 to $14 after six. But people have no complaints if the restaurant gives an early bird discount that cuts the price of the steak to $12 from $14. Since by hypothesis for the person who dines at seven the price is the same $14 under either scenario. People judge the first scenario as unfair and the second scenario not so unfair. The ethical manager can argue that these fairness norms of customers cannot be rationally justified. Sales managers may also argue that there are no universal norms of fairness. These arguments all miss the point, however. Sales managers are not moral philosophers. Their job is to serve the needs of the stockholders and the customers. Neither interest is served when the manager declares that the view of fairness held by the customers is irrational and refuses to honor their views on the matter.

This point is driven home by a real-life example. How notions of fairness impact on how consumers react to price differentiation (as this practice is called in marketing class) is presented by the Coca-Cola Company, which had invented a Coca-Cola dispenser that reacts automatically to temperature. That is, as the temperature goes up, the price of Coca-Cola goes up as well. When the CEO of Coca-Cola at that time, M. Douglas Ivester, announced the existence of the new dispenser in Brazil that was then reported in the *New York Times*,[2] the public reacted with outrage. Charging more for a Coke when it gets hot outside violated deeply held norms of fairness. Coca-Cola's competitor PepsiCo promised that it would never use such a dispenser.[3] Coca-Cola needed to backtrack, abandon its plans, and promise not to introduce the dispenser. The cost to the Coca-Cola company was in millions of dollars.

Moreover, the notion of fairness is not a cultural concept, although what counts as fair may vary from culture to culture. During the SARS crisis in China, there was a rumor in some cities that vinegar could protect one against SARS. Merchants greatly increased the price of vinegar in response. Most citizens believed that the merchants had engaged in unfair behavior. Price gouging is not simply a Western notion.

Finally, some considerations of fairness do seem to be objectively grounded. Managers ought not take advantage of the vulnerabilities of others when these vulnerabilities are not the responsibility of those who have them. Price gouging is wrong because it takes advantage of those who are made vulnerable by an act of nature (acts of God as they are often called). Even the libertarian Robert Nozick would not agree that the person who owned the only waterhole in the desert had a right to charge what he wanted. We take as an objective principle of fairness that people who are vulnerable through no fault of their own should not have their vulnerability exploited. We shall call this the "vulnerability principle."

Although the vulnerability principle seems acceptable, considerable disagreement exists as to whether someone is vulnerable through no fault of their own. For example, Norman Bowie gives the following situation to his MBA students: Suppose you are an antique dealer and are in Maine in search of antiques. You discover a farmer who is desperately in need of money because a drought has caused a crop failure. He has an Empire table worth $10,000 up for sale for $100.

Bowie then asks how many would pay $100 and say nothing (a proxy for thinking it not unfair). A huge majority would say nothing and pay the $100. Sometimes the class is unanimous on that issue. When asked what justifies taking advantage of the ignorance of the farmer, the class says it was the responsibility of the farmer to educate himself about the value of his possessions. When Bowie added detail after detail to show how difficult that would be for a Maine farmer, few in the class were swayed. (Interestingly, most of the class would not try to bargain with the farmer to lower the price even further as is customary in yard sales of that type.) This anecdote leads naturally to the following question.

▲ HOW SHOULD VULNERABLE CUSTOMERS ▲ BE TREATED AND WHAT COUNTS AS VULNERABILITY ANYWAY?

All customers are not equal in terms of sophistication or economic circumstances. A number of businesses exist that cater to vulnerable consumers. Check-cashing companies will cash your checks if you do not have a bank account – for a large fee. Bad credit? No credit? No problem. Firms exist to loan a person money at extraordinarily high rates of interest. One report indicated that interest rates in the "subprime market" as it is called can run between 300 percent and 2000 percent on an annualized basis.[4] For decades the subprime lending companies were small businesses. But in the last decade, Wall Street firms and big name banks have gotten into the business. Leading subprime mortgage security underwriters in 1999 included Lehman Brothers at $11.5 billion, Merrill Lynch at $6.9 billion, Bank of America at $6.2 billion, Greenwich Capital Markets at $6.2 billion, Prudential Securities at $6 billion, and Salomon Smith Barney at $5.7 billion.[5] Do such companies exploit the vulnerable or provide a legitimate service?

On the one hand, firms that provide these services argue that higher fees are justified by the increased risk. They also argue that if they did not cash checks or provide credit, no one else would. Rather than exploiting these people, they are providing a service they could not get elsewhere. Critics might accept this argument but argue that the check-cashing fees and the loan interest rates are still too high. But consider the comment of an attorney with Atlanta Legal Aid:

We've created a financial apartheid within society. Lenders claim the reason that the cost of these financial resources is so high is because the risks are tremendous. The whole shadow banking industry is riddled with abuses that have nothing to do with credit risk.[6]

Coercion and deception are some of these abuses. Let us invoke Immanuel Kant, as we did in chapter 3, to provide the moral argument against coercion and deception. Coercion and deception violate Kant's principle of respect for persons. Kant scholar Christine Korsgaard puts the point as follows:

> According to the Formula of Humanity, coercion and deception are the most fundamental forms of wrongdoing to others – the roots of all evil. Coercion and deception violate the conditions of possible assent, and all actions which depend for their nature and efficacy on their coercive character are ones that others cannot assent to ... Physical coercion treats someone's person as a tool; lying treats someone's reason as a tool. That is why Kant finds it so horrifying; it is a direct violation of autonomy.[7]

Charges of coercion and deception abound in the subprime lending industry. It is one thing if customers come to the lenders or respond to honest straightforward ads. Then the "we are providing a service" defense might make some sense. However, that often is not the case. For example, the *Business Week* report cites lenders who "goad low income homeowners into refinancing existing mortgages with new loans that carry such high rates, high fees, and hidden balloon payments that they virtually guarantee default and foreclosure."[8] For example, lenders have refinanced the poor out of 0 percent loans built by Habitat for Humanity into double-digit rate loans. Other abuses occur with loan consolidation loans. Rodney Foster, who lives in a small row house in Philadelphia, was behind on his Veterans Administration (VA) mortgage and other bills. Equicredit, a division of Bank of America Corporation, paid off the loan without his permission. The VA mortgage was for $30,000 and had an interest rate of 9.5%. Equicredit substituted a $43,200 loan at 12.05 percent and roughly 13 points in fees.[9] Equicredit hardly provided a service. Rather, they unjustly exploited the vulnerable. And when people fall behind on the subprime loans, heavy-handed tactics are used to collect on them. When a Navajo couple fell behind on about $700 on a 24 percent a year car loan, "they received a notice from the lender that grabbed their attention: a drawing of two burly repo men, one holding a sledgehammer and the other a gun standing over a borrower lying in a garbage can."[10] Such tactics stink legally as well as ethically. The couple won a $500,000 judgment.

What are the managers of check-cashing firms or these loan agencies obligated to do in these circumstances? They are morally permitted to receive a premium because of the additional risk. They must disclose fully and completely the terms of the loan. They are not morally permitted to deceive or coerce. In addition, we have as a fundamental moral principle that sales managers cannot take advantage of the vulnerable. In industries like subprime lending, where the sales manager knows that he or she is dealing with a vulnerable population, then he or she has a special obligation to try to have the product meet the need. For cases of the vulnerable, something like Holley's mutual benefit rule might be what is required. The sales manager does not need to point out to the vulnerable that a competitor can provide a product cheaper, but does need to provide the vulnerable with information about the product that will best provide for the person's need. Basically we are arguing for a level of paternalism with respect to the vulnerable that one would not expect and indeed would be unjustified with respect to the rational consumer. We will use this moral principle as we analyze a number of cases in what follows.

Other mainline businesses have a niche for the vulnerable. Consider an example provided by Joe Desjardins: He describes an example of a campaign "that depicts an elderly woman at the bottom of the stairs crying out, 'I've fallen and I can't get up.'" The targeted market for emergency call devices is elderly women living alone. Does this ad that depicts the woman who has fallen at the bottom of the stairs exploit the elderly? [11] Desjardins challenges the ethics of the ad on the ground that the portrayal of the woman plays on the fears or anxieties of older people.[12] However, we disagree. Fear of falling and becoming incapacitated when living alone is a genuine fear. Elderly people do fall more often, they are more likely to be incapacitated, and the consequences of such a fall when living alone could indeed be dire. The target marketer has a product that if purchased would ease or eliminate a fear that elderly people living alone do in fact have. We do not see what is wrong with this campaign, as it addresses the fears and anxieties of the customers.

Desjardins anticipates this defense and is not persuaded. He notes that vulnerability comes in many forms. Vulnerability occurs when there is some factor that predisposes a person to a greater risk of harm than what is faced by others. "Consumer vulnerability occurs when a person has an impaired ability to make an informed consent to the market exchange ... General vulnerability occurs when someone is susceptible to some specific physical, psychological, or financial harm."[13] Desjardins believes that all target marketing based on consumer vulnerability as he defines it is wrong and we agree. However, we do not think that the campaign aimed at the elderly women has "impaired ability to make an informed consent to the market exchange." Desjardins treats the case of the emergency call device as analogous to the case where funeral directors play on the grief and perhaps the guilt of the bereaved in order to sell them a more expensive funeral service than they can afford. We would argue that grief, especially when coupled with guilt, does impair the ability to make an informed consent. But being afraid of an incapacitating fall when living alone does not undermine informed consent. Neither does a life insurance ad that shows a person with a happy family and then shows that person out of the picture and asks, "Who will take care of them when you are gone?" Merely playing on the emotions does not always impair informed consent but rather certain emotional appeals can lead a consumer to do what an informed consumer would rationally do – namely buy some life insurance. The test cannot simply be whether or not the appeal to the target audience is based on the emotions.

Let us consider another example that has been a staple in the literature and has been discussed by Desjardins as well. A number of beer companies had a high profile campaign for malt liquor directed at inner-city blacks. One brand called PowerMaster by Heileman brewery was especially criticized, given the reality that inner-city blacks had very little power and the attempt to achieve power through PowerMaster made things worse rather than better. Naturally Desjardins condemned this campaign because it appealed to the emotion of powerlessness and the campaign undermined the ability of inner-city blacks to make a informed market choice. Business ethicist George Brenkert wrote the classic article on this case and he proposed a set of criteria for determining who counts as a vulnerable consumer with respect to making an informed market choice. Brenkert lists three kinds of vulnerability:

A person would be cognitively vulnerable if he or she lacked certain levels of ability to cognitively process information or be aware that certain information was being withheld or manipulated in deceptive ways.

A person would be motivationally vulnerable if he or she could not resist ordinary temptation and/or enticements due to his or her own individual characteristics.

A person would be socially vulnerable when their social situation renders them significantly less able than others to resist various enticements.[14]

Interestingly, with respect to Heileman he came to the opposite conclusion to Desjardins. He did not think that Heileman had undermined the ability of inner-city blacks to make an informed choice. However, he did think that the beer industry as a whole had undermined the ability of inner-city blacks to make an informed choice. Let us look at the criteria again and the reasons that Brenkert gave for not holding Heileman responsible. Inner-city blacks are neither cognitively nor motivationally vulnerable with respect to the Heileman ads. However, if that claim is true, and we think it is, then we think it would also hold true with respect to the beer industry in general. Brenkert does not provide any evidence to show cognitive or motivational vulnerability, even with respect to saturation alcohol ads that are sometimes found in the inner city. Thus, Brenkert's case must rest on social vulnerability. After all Brenkert cites many statistics showing the extent of alcohol consumption in inner-city black neighborhoods, the harm caused by alcohol abuse, and the fact that there is more beer advertising in inner-city black neighborhoods than in middle-class white neighborhoods. Those statistics are undeniable. But does the poverty and relative lack of power of inner-city blacks mean that their choices in the marketplace are not really free.

We think that both Desjardins and Brenkert put the focus of the ethical issue in the wrong place. They focus on whether the advertising campaign undermines autonomous market choice. On that criterion it is hard to say that it does, so it is hard to say that the marketing managers behaved unethically. But in what looks like an aside, Desjardins added another reason why the campaign was wrong. The marketers should have known that many inner-city blacks seek to deaden their despair with alcohol and this is an inappropriate use of the product. We think this puts the moral emphasis in the right place. What distinguishes the emergency call device from the PowerMaster campaign is that playing on the emotions of the elderly person living alone encourages them to make a purchase that truly benefits them. It is the same with a family breadwinner who does not have life insurance. Playing on that person's emotions encourages the purchase of life insurance that he or she ought to have. However, playing on the emotions of inner-city blacks encourages them to use a product to excess in a way that hurts them rather than benefits them, and the marketers know this to be the case. That is what makes the PowerMaster campaign wrong. It is knowledge on the part of the marketers that their targeted customers will likely abuse the product to their detriment. Certainly, a salesperson should not try to sell someone something that they know is likely to cause that person harm. This principle was established early on in this chapter. Thus, we conclude that with respect to the vulnerable, sales managers have special obligations that they do not have to rational consumers. They should not overcharge nor should they oversell, and they should certainly not try to sell the vulnerable products that there is good reason to believe will cause them harm.

While some may exploit the vulnerable, other firms will not serve the vulnerable at all. If you have too many claims, your insurance company can and probably will drop you. Is that fair? One of the most egregious instances of this with respect to employees occurs when firms fire disabled workers in order to reduce health-care costs. Here is what a study by Mercer Human Resource Consulting found: 27 percent of 723 companies surveyed dismiss employees as soon as they go on long-term disability and 24 percent dismiss them within a specified time after going on disability. Six to twelve months is the most common time frame.[15] The highlighted example in the *Wall Street Journal* account was Polaroid, whose assets are owned by Banc One. One of those fired was John Magenheimer, who had a cancerous tumor that was pressing against his heart removed. In order to get to the cancer, surgeons had to remove one of his ribs. Magenheimer implicitly raises the fairness question when he said, "How could Polaroid do this to me? For more than twenty years I gave them everything I had."[16]

We think Mr Magenheimer has made exactly the right point. What Polaroid did is unfair and it should also be made illegal. Furthermore, the vulnerable should be provided with essential services either by their employers or by government. If a company provides long-term disability insurance, it should not be allowed to fire people when they have to use it.

▲ TO WHAT EXTENT IS THE DIFFERENTIAL ▲ TREATMENT OF CUSTOMERS RIGHT?

Some customers spend much more money with a business than other customers. As a result they gain special privileges. Some of these privileges are accepted as morally correct while others are condemned as unfair. We will consider some examples of differential treatment to try to come up with some principles that would help determine when discrimination is unfair and when it is not.

Let us consider the airline industry. All major US airlines have a frequent flyer program that gives advantages to frequent flyers that are not available to non-frequent flyers. These benefits include a better choice of seats, free upgrades, and expedited security lines. Of course, you can pay for these privileges by buying a first-class or business class ticket. Most people have no problem with the upgrades and a better choice of seats. The underlying principle seems to be: If you pay more, you are entitled to more.

Expedited security lines are a bit more controversial. A terrorist attack, which is an act of war, caused the increased security measures. The basic moral intuition here is that in wartime, people should not use higher income to buy their way out of the burdens created by war. That is why buying one's way out of the draft in time of war is considered wrong. During the civil war, draft riots ensued when people were allowed to pay others to take their place. A vivid portrayal of the New York City draft riots can be seen in the recent Martin Scorsese film, *Gangs of New York*. During the Vietnam War in the 1960s the system of draft deferments in place was said to be unfair to the poor because many of them could not afford to be in college and thus gain a student deferment. The strength of this criticism was recognized and by the end of the war a lottery system was adopted. The security lines were caused by an act of war and there are issues of fairness in buying your way out of the waiting time.

Suppose you want to call the issuer of your credit card for some information about a charge against your account. An automated voice message asks for your credit card number. How soon you get connected to a live person is dependent on a number of factors including how much you charge against the card, how good your payment record is, and how much interest you are paying. Whether you are on hold for two minutes or for ten depends on how good a customer you are. Is that fair? Is being connected quicker a benefit to which the better customers are entitled or is waiting on line a burden which should fall on profitable and less profitable customers alike?

On the whole, we are uncomfortable with this recent trend. The trend has shifted from "The Customer is Always Right" to "Only the High-paying Customer Gets Service." Our intuition here seems close to the early bird special case at the restaurant discussed earlier. It does not seem unfair if a high-paying customer gets a perk. On the other hand, it seems unfair when a low-volume customer gets hit with a penalty – such as being put on hold for an inordinately long time. Sales managers need to give more thought to this issue.

▲ WHEN SHOULD CUSTOMERS' WANTS ▲ AND PREFERENCES BE OVERRIDDEN?

Telemarketing has been a huge industry in the United States and has been universally hated. The intrusion of unwanted phone calls – especially at meal times when, after all, people are most likely to be home, was so unpopular that the politicians finally did something. Once the federal government permitted a "no call" list, millions of Americans called in on the first day to get on the list and tens of millions have since registered their phone numbers. Yet the unwanted solicitations continue with junk mail through the post office and spam on the Internet. Marketers have vowed to increase the amount of junk mail and spam as a result of the new laws on telemarketing.

With respect to spam, some companies, especially those that have privacy seals, will allow a person to avoid receiving most spam by a process called opting out. Consumers opt out when they check a box indicating they do not want their information shared with others or have cookies put on their computers. Business fights legislation for a required opt-out system for spam. Europe has an even stronger opt-in system. An opt-in system requires that a person actually agrees to have cookies placed on his or her computer or to have his or her name sent to third parties. The vast majority of Americans do not want this stuff. Do sales managers have an obligation to honor the desires of most Americans on this issue?

Another huge annoyance is the substitution of mechanical devices for real people. Try to contact a business today by phone and speak directly with a real person. "Our options have changed. Please pay special attention. Push 1 for ..., Push 2 for ..., Push 3 for ..., etc." If your option is not available, tough luck. The airlines do this, the cable company does this, the utility companies do this, the credit card companies do this, the banks do this, doctors do this, and on and on and on. Customers hate it. Yet it continues. Clearly managers are ignoring the very clear wishes of their customers when they impose this inconvenience on them. It seems to us that business is required to justify doing something that customers do not want done.

Northwest Airlines is introducing a policy that will force customers to use an electronic check-in procedure. In other words, no more going up to a live person to get a boarding pass. Other airlines are in the process of doing the same thing. Machines are cheaper than people. A Northwest spokesperson indicated that each machine replaced 28 people. In these times, you have to be sympathetic with the airline industry and their desire to cut costs. However, Northwest does not have a computer that can handle hyphenated last names. As a result the credit card that can accommodate hyphens will not match the reservation that cannot. This prevents one from getting a boarding pass. Only recently did Northwest modify its system so that you could type in your confirmation number – a lengthy process – and receive your boarding pass.

With this heavy emphasis on costs, managers are showing over and over again that not only is the customer not right but that the customer will be forced to do it the manager's way. Is there an issue of coercion here? In the examples we have been considering the manager of a business is depriving us of choices we would have freely made if we could. Even the telemarketers are doing this because they are making us get up to answer the phone when we clearly would not want to if we knew a telemarketer was calling.

In a competitive market, this problem can sometimes be avoided when a business seeks a market niche to get customers that object to what the majority of businesses are doing. When the competitive market works in this way, we agree that the problem is solved. But often the competitive market cannot solve the problem. It is hard to imagine a successful start-up airline that can succeed on the basis that you can easily get a boarding pass from a live person, and there is no alternative possible in the telemarketing industry as the nature of the industry is to sell by getting you to answer the phone. The closest we came to a market response was devices to screen tele-marketers – caller ID, for example. However, citizens have spoken. These devices were not sufficient and now legislation has been passed. Whether it will pass Constitutional muster remains to be seen.

Of course, business does not need to acquiesce in every unpopular desire, even when the vast majority of people would want it done differently. For example, most people do not want to pay a fee to use an ATM machine. Is the view of the majority morally justified? (In the United Kingdom fees for ATM machines were so unpopular that legislation was passed forbidding them.) What would justify a bank in charging a fee for using an ATM machine? First, ATM machines cost money and it is not unreasonable for those who consume a resource to pay for it plus a reasonable profit. Second, there are alternative moderately convenient ways to get your money – from bank cashiers during normal business hours. In other words, paying for a service used and genuine alternatives are relevant moral criteria.

Note that the Northwest Airlines policy violates these conditions. ATM machines add to convenience by allowing you to get money 24 hours a day. They increase convenience, not decrease it, and thus charging a fee for increasing convenience is justified. Northwest will allow you to print out your boarding pass within 30 hours of the flight. That increases your convenience and is not only justified but provides a genuine service. Forcing you to use a machine at the airport, however, is not a convenience for the customer – especially if you have a hyphenated last name.

We suspect that the real goal behind the ignoring of customer preference is the desire to eliminate people as an expense. Here we have a number of cases where the wishes and interests of at least two stakeholder groups – the customers and the employees – are being sacrificed for the benefit of the stockholders. This attitude on the part of managers of always putting stockholders first has been strongly criticized on moral and prudential grounds in previous chapters. Since a business is a set of relationships among stake-holders, managers have an obligation to try to balance the interests of all the corporate stakeholders. However, it seems to many observers that managers are always giving priority to the stock-holders on these matters. As we argued in chapter 2, that is morally wrong.

▲ CONCLUSION ▲

This chapter has provided many examples where managers have violated their obligations to customers. We base that judgment on fairly universal grounds that indicate that coercion and deception are wrong and that exploitation of the vulnerable is unfair and wrong as well. In addition, we have defended the principle that sales managers and advertising managers should provide consumers with information about the product or service they could not reasonably have gotten themselves. With respect to the vulnerable we have maintained that sales managers have the additional burden of making sure that a product they sell cannot harm them and is reasonably designed to meet a genuine need of the vulnerable. We think that sales managers and advertisers ought to take a more paternalistic stand with the vulnerable. We have also criticized practices that repeatably subordinate the interests of the consumer to the interests of the stockholder. Special criticism has been levied on practices that subordinate more than the interests of one stakeholder group for the benefits of the stockholder. The customer may not be always right but he or she should be treated in a way that respects him or her as a person and, at least sometimes, makes his or her needs superior to the needs of the stockholder.

▲ NOTES ▲

1. This material is from David M. Holley, "Information Disclosure in Sales," *Journal of Business Ethics* 17 (1998), pp. 631–41.
2. Constance L. Hays, "Coke Tests Vending Unity That Can Hike Prices in Hot Weather," *New York Times* (October 28, 1999).
3. Ibid.
4. Dean Foust, "Easy Money," *Business Week* (April 24, 2000), p. 108.
5. Ibid.
6. Ibid.
7. Christine Korsgaard, *Creating the Kingdom of Ends* (Cambridge: Cambridge University Press, 1996), pp. 140, 141.
8. Foust, "Easy Money," p. 109.
9. Ibid., p. 110.
10. Ibid., p. 112.
11. Joseph Desjardins, *Business Ethics* (Englewood Cliffs, NJ: McGraw Hill, 2003), p. 168.
12. Ibid.

13. Ibid., p. 169.
14. George Brenkert, "Marketing to Inner-City Blacks: PowerMaster and Moral Responsibility," *Business Ethics Quarterly* 8 (1998), p. 6.
15. Joseph Pereira, "To Save on Health-Care Costs, Firms Fire Disabled Workers," *Wall Street Journal* (July 14, 2003), pp. A1, A8.
16. Ibid., p. A1.

chapter five

Supply Chain Management and Other Issues

Most books on business ethics, when discussing stakeholder management, focus on the stockholders, employees, and to a lesser extent on customers and the local community. Marketing ethics texts put the emphasis on the customers. The local community will be the focus of chapter 6. However, there are many other stakeholders even when "stakeholders" are narrowly defined as "groups whose support is necessary to the survival of the firm." Business schools treat suppliers very seriously, and a relatively new term "supply chain management" has come into the business school lexicon. There are a number of important ethical issues that arise with respect to managing the supply chain. One of the most important concerns issues of responsibility.

Other stakeholder groups are ignored both by business ethicists and by business schools. The media, especially investigative reporting, is a formidable foe when it has a story involving corporate wrongdoing that will play well with the public. Business leaders ignore the media at their peril. We shall argue that the standard competitive analysis is too narrow and that the media should be classified as a competitor of a certain sort, raising all the ethical issues of how we should treat competitors.

Yet another important stakeholder group is government agencies. Their support is certainly necessary to the survival of the firm. This became most obvious as government grappled with the effects of all the corporate scandals that emerged in 2002–3. A government decision to prosecute put Arthur Andersen out of business. The impact of government on business pushes business toward a compliance-based ethical stance as opposed to a values-based stance. Limiting managerial ethics to compliance-based ethics is itself, as we shall see, an ethical issue. Just as the government passes laws to regulate business behavior, businesses lobby government to pass laws favorable to business or to limit the onerous effect of regulations on business. Lobbying government officials raises central issues of fairness – especially in light of the power of business compared to other stakeholder groups.

In this chapter we will also say some things about ethical dealings with non-governmental organizations (NGOs). NGOs are roughly equivalent with not-for-profit groups that have a single issue or a limited number of ethical issues that each wants addressed. The Sierra Club, Amnesty International, and the International Labor Organization are all NGOs. Although NGOs do not have a lot of influence in the United States, they are extremely powerful in Europe. For example, Greenpeace was able to defeat environmental decisions made by Royal Dutch Shell, even though those decisions were perfectly legal and arguably perfectly ethical as well. US companies doing business abroad need to consider the role of NGOs and decide how to deal with them in an ethical fashion.

▲ SUPPLY CHAIN MANAGEMENT ▲

Ethical issues regarding supply chain management are relatively recent. They have been brought to the attention of the public by NGOs in cooperation with the media. The most volatile supply chain ethical issue has been sweatshops. The campaign against sweatshops was orchestrated by Charles Kernaghan, president of the National Labor Coalition – an organization of 25 labor unions. In 1996, Kernaghan appeared before a Congressional committee. His charges included a claim that Katie Lee Gifford's clothing line was made by 13- and 14-year-olds working 20-hour days in factories in Central America. Kernaghan made it possible for some of the teenagers from Central America to appear before the committee. One of the young teenage girls displayed a sweater with a Liz Claiborne logo.[1] Child labor, obscenely low wages, and dangerous working conditions all play well on the seven o'clock news and are genuine moral issues.

To see the issues involved, we need to consider carefully the notion of moral responsibility. Normally one can only be held morally responsible for what one does. And even when a person does something wrong, there can be mitigating or excusing circumstances. Thus, in an attempt to help someone, one might injure them instead. Usually one is not morally blameworthy for the injury (although one might still be legally liable). One can also be mistaken, as when someone gives a thirsty person a drink, not realizing the water is contaminated. Again one is not usually morally responsible for the person getting ill. Ignorance and unintentional harmful consequences usually get one off the moral hook. But not always. If a person should not have been ignorant, or if he or she were reckless in trying to help someone, then he or she would be morally responsible. We are all familiar with the lame excuse, "I only did it because I was drunk." Well, as Aristotle pointed out centuries ago, you are responsible for getting drunk. But note that in this discussion we were always speaking of the person who did the act trying to determine whether he or she was morally responsible or not.

But when is one responsible for the act of another? After all, the basic argument here is that in some instances management is responsible for the actions of its supplier. There are some legal parallels here. Parents are sometimes held responsible for the actions of their children. More commonly under the doctrine of respondent superior, business firms are held responsible for the actions of their employees. The basis for the latter view is that the employee is the agent of the management and is thus acting on behalf of management. Thus management should supervise its employees and, should they fail to do so and bad consequences result, then management can be held morally responsible.

The keys here are agency and duty to supervise. The supplier has traditionally not been considered an agent for the firm it supplies. The supplier has been treated as an independent business. This lack of agency has implied that there is no duty to supervise. What has changed in the public's mind in the sweatshop cases is that companies that sell apparel and sporting goods have an obligation to supervise those who manufacture the goods for them. Suppose one agrees that the public's perception has changed in the way that we have described. Does that mean the public is morally correct in its perception?

Historically, those who sold apparel and sporting goods also manufactured them. In order to lower costs, firms like Nike and Liz Claiborne no longer manufacture the products they sell. So they stepped out of manufacturing, contracted the manufacturing piece out, and contracted with suppliers to make goods for them. Presumably, these contracts contained specifications for what was to be delivered. Why limit the contract to the product itself? Why not specify the conditions under which it is made and include specifications as to how labor is to be treated? After all, the product will have Nike's name on it and thus Nike should take responsibility for the quality of the product.

However, the employees of the supplier are in no way Nike's. Indeed, only a small number of the supplier's employees may work on Nike products. Although it is reasonable to say that Nike should be responsible for the quality of its product, why should it also be held responsible for situations that have nothing to do with product quality?

In a classic US legal case *Henningsen* v. *Bloomfield Motors*, the Henningsens sought damages from a car crash that was caused by a defective part in the automobile. Chrysler was the manufacturer of the car who sold it to the Chrysler dealer, Bloomfield Motors, who then sold it to Mr Henningsen. Mrs Henningsen, who was driving the defective car when it crashed, had no contractual relationship with any party. In legal terms there was no privity of contract with Mrs Henningsen. Indeed, there was no privity of contract with Mr Henningsen. Chrysler argued that its responsibilities ended when it sold the car to Bloomfield Motors. The court rejected Chrysler's arguments. After all, Chrysler was the cause of the defective car. Its responsibility thus extended to those who would use the product even though they had not actually bought the car from Chrysler. Indeed Mrs Henningsen, the injured party, had not purchased the car from anyone. Thus, one can be morally responsible to parties with whom one does not stand in a direct relationship.

But this analysis will still not get us quite what we want. After all the dispute that the NGOs had with Nike was not with the quality of Nike's sportswear. It was with the conditions under which Nike's supplier manufactured the sportswear. A claim that Nike should be responsible for the working conditions of the suppliers' employees is to extend the realm of responsibility beyond the doctrine in Henningsen.

What arguments might be given for extending the realm of responsibility in this way? A utilitarian might argue that, given the moral wrong to be corrected, the most efficient solution, all things considered, is that the powerful company that holds the purse strings be responsible for their suppliers. The bigger and richer you are, the more responsibility you have for your supply chains. The richer and more powerful players have the means to correct the problem and it would be most efficient if they were the ones to right the moral wrong. It was just this kind of utilitarian argument that carried the day when product liability law shifted to strict liability. Manufacturers were held liable even if they were not at fault.

Another approach is to make the argument on the basis of a violation of human rights. In this argument, a marketer should not sell goods by suppliers who have violated human rights. The moral violations of the supplier on this view contaminate the actions of the marketer as well. This argument has been especially effective in Europe. The most visible use of the argument is the campaign against sweatshops.

Sweatshops, it is alleged, violate the human rights of the supplier's employees. There are three main areas of ethical concern: (1) coercion in the form of forced overtime and locking employees in; (2) inadequate safety standards; and (3) lack of a living wage. For example, Denis Arnold, in his article on the topic, argues that labor practices in sweatshops violate Articles 3, 4, and 5 of the United Nations Universal Declaration of Human Rights, which prohibit forced labor, indentured servitude, corporal punishment of employees by supervisors, and seriously unsafe working conditions. Many sweatshop managers also violate Article 23, Section 4, which prohibits the termination of employees for organizing or joining a union. Article 23, Section 2 provides a basis for the prohibition of discrimination and Article 24 provides a basis for arguing that sweatshops are morally required to pay wages adequate for a dignified standard of living without extensive overtime hours.[2]

We admit that there are those who do not think the practices of sweatshops violate human rights. Those who reject the argument that the behavior of the sweatshop managers is morally wrong cite a number of facts as premises for their conclusion. People in underdeveloped countries are begging for employment in the sweatshops; they are hardly coerced. The wages of the sweatshops are very low compared to US standards but often exceed the wages of professionals, such as teachers and even doctors, in some of the countries where sweatshops are located. Moreover, an attempt to raise wages above market-determined rates would only make matters worse. It would increase the cost of labor which would further increase unemployment (the countries where sweatshops are located usually have high unemployment) and make the lives of those who do not work in the sweatshops even worse off. What is moral about adding to the income of those who are already better off by subtracting from those who are worse off.[3]

Sweatshops' critics have responses to each of these arguments. First, there are genuine cases of coercion. Mostly the coercion concerns forced overtime. In their paper on this topic, Denis Arnold and Norman Bowie cite the following instances of coercion: In Bangladesh, factory workers report that they are expected to work virtually every day of the year. Overtime pay, although a legal requirement, is often not paid and employees who refuse to work overtime are fired. An El Salvadoran government study found that workers were required to work overtime even when their health was threatened. On some occasions overtime work extended so far into the night that workers had to sleep over in the factories, which did not have adequate (or any) lodging facilities.[4]

Yet another form of coercion involves forcing employees to meet production quotas. Read the report of a 26-year-old worker who sews steering-wheel covers at a Mexican *maquila*:

> We have to work quickly with our hands, and I am responsible for sewing 20 steering wheel covers per shift. After having worked for nine years at the plant, I now suffer from an injury in my right hand. I start out the shift okay, but after about three hours of work, I feel a lot of sharp pain in my fingers. It gets so bad that I can't hold the steering wheel correctly. But still the supervisors keep pressuring me to reach 100% of my production. I can reach about 70% of what they ask for. These pains began a year ago and I am not the only one who has suffered from them. There are over 200 of us who have hand injuries and some have lost movement in their hands and arms. The company has fired over 150 people in the last year for lack of production. Others have been pressured to quit.[5]

A charge that defenders of sweatshops either ignore or downplay is the existence of violations of even minimum safety standards. This problem received worldwide attention in 1993, when a fire at the Kader Industrial Toy Company in Thailand killed 200 workers (mostly women) and injured over 400 others. In Bangladesh there have been 17 fires that have resulted in fatalities since 1995. A fire in 2001 at Chowdhury Knitwears claimed 52 lives.[6] Frequently the death toll is high because exit doors have been locked or chained shut so that workers could not leave the facility. There is no economic reason or marketplace pressure that would justify locking employees into facilities, which increases loss of life in the event of a fire.

The debate around a living wage is far more complicated and cannot be examined in detail here. What is needed is some definition of a living wage that provides a minimum for subsistence.[7] Let us assume that such a definition can be provided. Multinationals should honor the minimum wage laws of the countries in which they operate. Often they do not. Managers should also realize that a healthy, reasonably well-fed, reasonably well-housed employee is more productive than one who lacks these traits. Often the increased costs in insuring that these conditions exist are more than offset by the increased productivity of the workforce. Finally, some evidence shows that an increase in wages does not necessarily cause a rise in unemployment.[8] If these arguments are correct, sweatshops' critics cannot be dismissed as impractical idealists. Since human rights can be honored by multinationals, they ought to be honored by them.

Suppose we accept as fact that many practices of sweatshops violate internationally recognized human rights and that these sweatshops are wrong to do so. That still leaves open the question whether Nike, Liz Claiborne, and others are morally responsible for the behavior of suppliers.

Interestingly, American companies are now being sued for complicity in human rights violations by governments in countries where they do business. The US Court of Appeals for the Ninth Circuit reversed a District Court dismissal of violation of human rights charges against Union Oil Company of California (Unocal). The alleged violations took place in Myanmar (formerly known as Burma). Unocal was involved in a natural gas project with other companies, including Myanmar Oil and Gas Enterprise. On the basis of evidence presented at trial, the court concluded that the Myanmar military was providing security for the project and that Unocal was aware of that fact. The court also concluded that Unocal knew that the Myanmar military was committing human rights violations in conjunction with the project. The fact that Unocal had such knowledge was sufficient for the court to have the case tried for liability under the Alien Tort Claims Act of 1789. In the absence of that law, there would be no legal case against Unocal.

These court cases are important as the *New York Times* recognized when it devoted a large article to the subject in its June 15, 2003, Sunday edition under the title, "Showdown for a Tool in Rights Lawsuits." In the article the philosophical issue is succinctly put. As William S. Dodge, an international law professor at the Hastings College of Law, said:

There are plenty of repressive regimes around the world, and there are plenty of multinationals that do business with them. The question is, how far can a corporation like Unocal go in cooperating with such a regime before the company bears some legal responsibility?[9]

Substitute "moral" for "legal" and we have our issue.

By parity of reasoning, Nike and others became aware of the fact that their suppliers violated human rights while manufacturing the products they sold. They are not responsible in any way for companies who violate human rights but supply them with products or stand in other business relations to them. However, they can and should demand that their suppliers honor universally accepted human rights. Otherwise there is complicity in human rights violations and that is unethical even if the Alien Tort Claims Act does not apply to them. This complicity is based on the fact that the supplier is an agent for the distributor, the distributor has a supervisory relationship with the supplier, and, as Robert Frederick has pointed out, the distributors should prevent their agents or business relationships from causing harm. If the analysis above is correct, the multinational bears moral responsibility when it is involved in a business relationship with a government or other business which it knows or ought to know is involved in human rights violations (causing harm) *in the business relationship*.

Whatever, the merits of the ethical case, after considerable public scrutiny Nike and others changed their stance. A set of international industry standards was adopted, and many firms belong to the Fair Labor Association. This association was founded in 1997 and is a sweatshop monitoring group. However, until recently, audits under the FLA and other auditing groups were not made public. In 2003 that changed, as a dozen members of the FLA agreed to public release of the audits.[10] Even if the philosophical grounds for the extension of responsibility to one's suppliers are still uncertain, world opinion has certainly moved in the direction of holding companies morally responsible for the human rights violations of its suppliers.

Another area in which the public is demanding more responsibility is on the environmental front. In fact it would not be unfair to summarize supply chain business ethics as the ethics of making sure that suppliers act in accord with human rights and that they be supportive of the environmental policy of the companies to which they supply goods and services. Several examples support this observation on the environmental front. Many of these examples come from the food industry.

For example, considerable pressure is being put on McDonald's to improve both the quality of fast food and the impact of their operations on the environment.[11] One concern of many environmentalists is the growth promotion antibiotics that are given to cattle. This enables the beef to grow faster. Approximately 20 million pounds of antibiotics are given yearly to US cattle, pigs, and chickens. The concern of the medical community is that the overuse of animals' drugs will create super bacteria. These super bacteria will then infect human beings when the meat is eaten. These super bacteria will be drug-resistant and would present a serious danger to the human population. McDonald's simply told its suppliers that it would no longer buy meat containing the antibiotics. These antibiotics have already been banned in Europe.

In some cases, the demands on suppliers come directly from the corporations themselves without the intervention of an aroused public. Starbucks is buying more organic and shade-grown coffee.[12] The responsibilities of managers to the environment are of sufficient importance that they receive considerable attention in chapter 6 where sustainability is discussed.

▲ MANAGING THE NEWS MEDIA ▲

The media is a business in its own right. This statement may seem obvious, but reporting the news is also considered a profession. A defining characteristic of a profession is that it is not simply driven by money. The main function of the news media at its ideal level is to discover the truth or to report the news as accurately as one can. Investigative reporting, such as that on *Sixty Minutes* or *Dateline*, tries to bring to light the bad deeds of government officials, sports celebrities, Hollywood stars, and, of course, business people. A common criticism of the news media these days is that its professional obligations have been swamped by the desire to succeed as a business, to make money.

This transition creates a dilemma for the moral manager. Should the news media be treated as a profession or as an adversary? How the news media ought to be treated depends in part on what they are. Even if the news media is now frequently an adversary, that does not mean that a manager is free to treat it any way he or she wants to.

Even among business competitors, there are rules of conduct – both explicit and implied – as to how competitors are to be treated. Stealing the intellectual property of another business is considered immoral. The reverse engineering of a competitor's product so that you might improve your own is not considered immoral. There are plenty of gray areas as well. What should you do if your competitor leaves the details of a competitive bid in the bar and you discover it?

Sometimes a manager is thrust into the news because of some event his company is involved with. Oil spills get companies in the news. The advice of legal counsel often is to say little and certainly to say nothing that can be used against you in court. But is deception or even the avoidance of the truth either ethical or even good business? The CEO of Ashland Oil, John Hall, faced this dilemma after an Ashland Oil tank ruptured and spilled oil into the Monongahela River near Pittsburgh one cold night in January 1988. As Hall flew to Pittsburgh to face the press, he knew that the tank was made from 30-year-old steel, that it had not been tested by the best method available, and that there was some question as to whether Ashland Oil had obtained the proper permits. Should he discuss those issues in the news conference and should he take questions – knowing that the press would be hostile?[13] He also needed to decide if Ashland Oil should formally apologize for the spill.

Hall chose to address the issues, saying what was known and what was not known, and he decided to take questions. He did not seem too confident, especially when answering questions. Nonetheless he was given high marks by the Pittsburgh media. The headline in the Pittsburgh Gazette was "Ashland Oil Scores High on Public Relations." Of course, honesty did not let Ashland Oil escape investigations and lawsuits. However, in one case the judge made it clear that he did not impose the maximum fine on Ashland because of Ashland's honest handling of the issue. Moreover, when the infamous *Exxon Valdez* oil spill occurred a little more than a year later, Exxon was compared unfavorably to Ashland. Exxon CEO Rawls never did visit the site and only belatedly sent a tape apologizing for the incident. The behavior of Exxon was widely considered a public relations disaster and Exxon came in for ethical criticism as well.

Is the lesson that should be taken from this discussion always to be completely transparent with the press? Certainly, transparency is an ethical ideal, but it is not always morally obligatory. Suppose Hall had been told that he would be interviewed for an hour by *Sixty*

Minutes. Should he have agreed and been so open if he had agreed? Not necessarily. After all, the actual Pittsburgh news conference was broadcast in its entirety. An interview is almost never broadcast in its entirety. And the investigative reporter can pick and choose which comments of the manager are to be reported or aired on TV. A live news conference is not as subject to manipulation as an interview. Different standards of transparency in the two cases are not unethical. What ethics requires depends in part on context, and the smart manager cannot be naïve about the news media.

Having said that, lying is still wrong. It is also usually bad business because the lie is almost always discovered. Transparency in a news conference situation – even in a hostile environment – is usually both morally and prudentially superior. If a company has harmed a community then they will suffer financial damage whether they admit it or not. Compliance officers know that as a general rule it is better to cooperate with government investigators. We submit that the same rule makes sense in dealing with the media as well. However, there is no moral obligation to submit oneself as a manager or one's company to an interview situation where the manager does not have significant control over how the interview can be used. This is especially true with investigative reporters, who are clearly adversaries during the interview session. As for prudence, there is debate as to whether a refusal to submit to the interview is better or worse. If a manager submits, he will probably be made to look bad. If he does not submit to the interview, his refusal will make him look bad. But his refusing in the situation described would not be a moral wrong.

▲ NGOs ▲

American managers have less experience with non-governmental organizations than their European counterparts. Nonetheless, we should realize that over one third of the membership of Corporate Social Responsibility Europe (CSR Europe) consists of American companies. NGOs are devoted to a social cause that they wish to advance. NGO members tend to be passionate believers in their cause and are unsympathetic with management's obligation to balance the interests of the various corporate stakeholders. The NGO wants its cause to have absolute priority. If challenged, they would point out that other stakeholders push their interests at the expense of other stakeholders. Why should NGOs be any different, they ask? One answer might be that NGOs claim the moral high ground yet they behave just like any regular business competitor to advance their goals. Two incidents illustrate this situation.

The H. B. Fuller Company sold a glue in Central America that was often sold illegitimately to street children. The street children used the glue to get high and thus eased the physical and psychological pain in their lives. However, the glue was addictive and caused severe brain damage. The legitimate consumers of the glue were the owners of small shoe-repair shops. However, some of the shoe repairmen sold the glue to street children for approximately 5 cents. Other street children stole the glue. The name of the glue was Resistol and the addicted street children became known as Resistoleros. H. B. Fuller tried a number of tactics to prevent the illegitimate use of the product – from treating it as a social problem on which they expended human and financial resources to finally withdrawing the product from the market. H. B. Fuller decided to leave the market on July 17, 1992. Speculation abounded that the cause for withdrawing from the market was a forthcoming interview with CEO Tony Andersen on NBC's *Dateline. Dateline* broadcast the story in that September. One year later *Dateline* returned to Honduras and discovered that H. B. Fuller still sold the glue in Honduras and the rest of Central America although only in industrial-size metal drums. *Dateline* insisted that Fuller had promised to get out of the market – period. Fuller was also under some pressure from a local Minnesota NGO, the Coalition on Resistoleros. Fuller's headquarters and several of its facilities are in Minnesota.

Fuller countered that they had only intended to stop selling glue in the kind of container that had been the subject of the abuse. Moreover, they were doing audits of their industrial customers to make sure that these customers were not ordering more glue than was needed for legitimate purposes. With respect to both the media and the NGOs, Fuller's initial strategy had been cooperation. However, after the second NBC *Dateline* report, Fuller's stance in both cases was to be far less cooperative. With respect to the Coalition on Resistoleros, Fuller had offered to meet with the group and its leader, Annie Baker, on a number of occasions. The invitations were never accepted. In the July/August 1993 issue of *Business Ethics,* Baker made a number of charges against Fuller. Significantly, *Business Ethics* had praised and even honored H. B. Fuller in the past for its progressive work with respect to the environment, the treatment of its employees, and its charitable contributions to the community. The Baker editorial in *Business Ethics* was too much. In a reply published in the November/December issue, Senior Vice-President Dick Johnson responded. Johnson's response raised a significant ethical issue not often addressed when an NGO or media representative attacks an industry or even a company on a matter of ethics. The tendency of the public is to question the motives and integrity of the company but not to raise questions regarding the motives and integrity of its accusers. In his editorial Johnson explicitly addressed this question:

> To be fair the spotlight should shine on all of us alike – Baker included. Is it socially responsible for self-appointed "authorities" to manipulate information and the media, merchandise falsehoods, and promote actions unsupported by the facts – all under the guise of helping the children? Is reputation bashing more important than ethics? What ethical standards are applied to groups and individuals like Baker?

After the second *Dateline* program, CEO Tony Andersen was angry. In a letter to employees Andersen wrote:

> The recent *Dateline* NBC broadcast was the final straw. It's time we stand up and say, "Enough!" We're disappointed and dissatisfied with the sensational, trivial, emotional, and grossly inaccurate portrayal the media has given to this serious issue. And we've had enough of the loudly voiced but unfounded claims of our critics who repeatedly espouse simplistic solutions without factual foundation.

In addition, Dick Johnson wrote an angry three-page letter to NBC News President Andrew Lack. In that letter he argued that NBC had misrepresented issues, had ignored facts, and, alluding to previous staged events by *Dateline*, asked pointedly whether an excerpt showing a street vendor pouring glue from a jar to a bag was staged. Most importantly, Fuller maintained that NBC had never proved that it was Resistol that was being sniffed. Following Fuller's departure from that niche of the market, its competitor, the German company Hankel, filled the gap.

Fuller now had a double-barreled ethical problem. First, it had to continue to address the substance abuse problem in Central America. Second, it had to deal with hostile reports from NGOs and the media, reports that Fuller believed to be unfair. How should a company respond in a way that is both ethical and protects its reputation that is so important to the bottom line? Before addressing this question, let us turn to our other case.

The other case involves Royal Dutch Shell and the *Brent Spar*. *Brent Spar* was part of an oil rig that Royal Dutch Shell had intended to sink in the North Atlantic. They had followed international law, made an environmental impact study and had the permission of the British government. The procedure was deemed efficient and safe. Greenpeace, however, took strong exception. They later admitted that they were wrong about the amount of contaminants in the rig. However, Greenpeace managed a brilliant public relations campaign that completely outmaneuvered Royal Dutch Shell. The tide of public opinion turned, boycotts of Shell were effective, and on the continent some Shell stations were firebombed. Greenpeace did not approve of the violence, but they proved to be tough adversaries. The Green Party in Germany was strong politically and it put enough pressure on the German government that the German Chancellor reneged on his support. Eventually Royal Dutch Shell agreed not to sink the *Brent Spar* and accepted an offer from Norway to store it in a Norwegian fjord. The British government under John Major was furious, thinking it had been betrayed by all parties. Royal Dutch Shell had suffered a major defeat at the hands of a radical environmental group.

Not long after, Royal Dutch Shell was also criticized by activists concerned with a violation of human rights. In this case NGOs faulted Shell for not intervening in Nigeria to try to save the life of Ken Saro-Wiwa, an activist from the Ogani area of Nigeria who was a leader in protests against Shell and the Nigerian government. Saro-Wiwa had been convicted by a military court for inciting the murder of a number of fellow tribesmen. All impartial observers had serious reservations about the fairness of the trial and the penalty. Nonetheless, Royal Dutch Shell had a policy of non-interference in political affairs and refused to intervene. Saro-Wiwa was executed and Royal Dutch Shell was subjected to worldwide criticism. As a result of the *Brent Spar* incident and the criticism of its behavior in Nigeria, Royal Dutch Shell began a systematic rethinking of its culture and its responsibilities as a corporate citizen.

Of particular interest to us here is how Royal Dutch Shell ought to deal with NGOs. What is the moral and prudent strategy for dealing with NGOs like Greenpeace? Royal Dutch Shell, as well as several other European companies, has decided to engage in "constructive dialog" with NGOs. Ethically, it is usually better to have dialog with those with whom one disagrees than have confrontation and conflict. The peaceful or negotiated resolution of disputes is morally superior to conflict. However, the resolution of disputes depends on the goodwill of both sides. Managers should realize that a cause represents the very being of an NGO. The cause is their product line so to speak. Thus, there is a self-interest bias in having the cause continue rather than resolving it. Companies should also realize that NGOs are willing and able to act strategically. They prefer a cause that will get them good press and "support dollars." Recently, scholars have been directing their attention to the fact that some companies are more likely to be under attack by the media and NGOs than other companies. Size is one variable. A good reputation to protect is another variable. Nike could not afford to have its reputation and thus its brand weakened by allegations of sweatshop conditions. Neither could the other major sportswear or apparel makers. NGOs were not unaware of this circumstance. Are NGOs behaving unethically in exploiting this fact? Perhaps, but that does not change the managerial problem – dealing with it. Besides, why do some large companies escape? Wal-Mart has been virtually untouched by all this despite its size and reputation.

We emphasize that we are not completely impugning the motives of NGOs, nor are we arguing that managers should not seek to cooperate with them. We are merely pointing out the impediments to resolution and urging managers to have another strategy for dealing with an NGO that prefers confrontation to negotiated settlements. In any case, the prudent and ethical manager will make sure that he or she has a solid case for decisions that are ethically sensitive and will make sure that there has been complete transparency about the objectives of the company and the means for meeting them. The ethical manager should also realize that the scrutiny of the press and NGOs does put pressure on less scrupulous companies to conform to higher standards of ethical behavior. In this respect, both the investigative media and NGOs play a legitimate role in improving corporate ethical behavior. On the other hand, students of competitive analysis need to take a broader notion of competition; there is product competition and there is information or public relations competition. The media or an NGO can be a competitor in the public relations arena and be every bit as tough as a product competitor. Exxon is a competitor of Royal

Dutch Shell, but in another sense of competition so is Greenpeace and *Sixty Minutes*. Often the ethics of dealing with NGOs or the investigative media is similar to what is ethically required in dealing with one's more traditional competitors.

▲ DEALING ETHICALLY WITH ▲ GOVERNMENT

Another stakeholder that receives little attention in traditional business ethics is the government. Surely the government is a stakeholder when stakeholders are defined as groups that can affect the survival of the firm. The government acts positively to enforce business contracts and enforces the laws against illegitimate business practices. Many of the allegations of misleading advertising are not brought to the Federal Trade Commission by consumers but rather by competitors. Lack of government enforcement of the law would lead to a situation in which the bad drives out the good. And the government is able to deliver a death sentence to a corporation that carries illegitimate conduct too far. A successful government prosecution against Arthur Andersen led to the demise of that firm, and the government's punishment of Enron by barring it from energy trading effectively destroyed that company as well.

Moreover, the government specifically takes the ethical conduct of companies into account when it pursues a company on legal grounds. For example, when Beechnut Nutrition Company celebrated its deception of state and federal authorities in disposing of adulterated apple juice, the federal authorities went after both the company and its top management, imposing convictions and severe fines on both. On the other hand, the previously mentioned co-operative behavior of Ashland Oil was explicitly taken into account by the judge in levying fines against Ashland Oil. This conduct is officially sanctioned in the 1991 Federal Sentencing Guidelines that require judges to increase the penalties against convicted companies that did not have ethical compliance programs in place to prevent corporate wrongdoing. It also requires judges to reduce the penalties for companies that did have an effective ethics program in place.

At a more general level, business must be concerned when unethical behavior by many in an industry results in calls for extensive government regulation – something that is nearly always opposed by business. As financial fraud and manipulation in one company after another became evident in 2002, the government responded with the Sarbanes–Oxley Act that vastly increased the reporting requirements on corporations, increased the list of prohibited activities, and increased the penalties for unethical and now illegal conduct. Even critics of corporate conduct admit that these regulations may be burdensome and overly broad. There is a saying that regulations enacted swiftly are not usually good regulations. Sarbanes–Oxley serves as a reminder to corporations that widespread corporate misconduct will result in a strong reaction from government and that the resulting legislation will be expensive and burdensome for those corporations that are usually ethical in their business conduct as well as for those that are not. Voluntary ethical conduct on the part of business is superior both morally and prudentially to a situation where government is forced to respond quickly to widespread corporate misconduct.

It should be noted that Sarbanes–Oxley was passed despite the lobbying power of business. Indeed, many provisions of Sarbanes–Oxley were similar to provisions that had already been defeated earlier as a result of business lobbying. The reform proposals of Arthur Levitt, former head of the Securities and Exchange Commission, were constantly defeated by business interests. The Public Oversight Board's funding was suspended in 2000 and it went out of business in 2001. It has returned with a vengeance under Sarbanes–Oxley. However, the view of many in the public and among business ethicists is that in reality the government's bark is far worse than its bite. It really takes a scandal of major proportions to pass legislation that is truly inimical to business. Indeed, with the exception of laws protecting employees against discrimination and sexual harassment, as well as laws protecting those with disabilities, the regulation of business is much stricter in other developed countries than it is in the United States. The chief explanation for this state of affairs is the powerful lobbying influence of business unchecked by the influence of labor or NGOs.

Are there any moral limits on the lengths that business should go in protecting themselves from government regulation or in gaining "favors" on the part of government? A Congressman writes provisions favoring a particular company or industry into a bill that has otherwise huge popular support. Other Congressmen support the bill because they support the overall bill even if they would reject these provisions. And for the same reason the President signs it. Is it wrong for a business to intentionally adopt this strategy? At one level we would argue that it is wrong. A business should gain an advantage on the merits of the overall argument, which normally means the advantage should arguably be in the public interest rather than in the interest of the firm alone. As we have seen throughout this book, a sign of unethical conduct is getting an exception for oneself that one is unwilling to grant others or that cannot be publicly advocated. Under this strategy the firm succeeds only because the legislators desire something else more than they do in rejecting the request. An advantage gained in this way is not ethical.

However, if everyone else is behaving unethically, does a company have a right not to behave ethically either? In other words, this is a classic public goods/prisoner's dilemma problem. If a business does not seek to gain an advantage in this way and its competitors do, then the "ethical" business is at a competitive disadvantage. Thus, everyone tries to get provisions that protect it and the public good suffers as a result.

What can and should be done? Urging companies to forgo their self-interest in the political arena is probably to ask for too much. Any company that did so would engage in an act of supererogation – analogous to a soldier who jumps on a grenade and sacrifices his own life for others. It is the responsibility of voters in a democracy to punish those who put special business interests ahead of the public good. However, to shift the burden in that way is too easy for business. Business managers have an obligation to seek industry cooperation for standards of good practice. If there can be standards of good business in supply chain management, there can also be standards of good business in relations between business and government.

There is one other ethical and prudential argument on behalf of business restraint in dealing with government. Our system of capitalism rests on the permission of the governed. As pointed out in chapter 2, the obligation of managers to be concerned with shareholder wealth is a public policy decision. If the fulfillment of that obligation does not lead to the public good, then society always has the option to change it;[14] that is the prudential piece. Business people and managers of business have enjoyed high prestige for a generation – approximately 25 years. However, that has not always been the case. In the 1960s the prestige of business was at a low point and young people were attracted to the professions, government service, and teaching. As the never-ending list of business scandals continues into late 2003, one wonders whether the tide is about to turn again, with the prestige of business and business executives plunging.

On the ethical side, there is the argument from gratitude, as business already receives great benefits from government – despite the tendency of business to disparage government. Government enforces business contracts, provides the infrastructure that makes business possible, provides for a stable currency, and enacts monetary and fiscal policy that is in the interest of business. Court decisions have given business free-speech rights comparable to those given to individuals. When a business takes advantage of these benefits and then moves its headquarters to Bermuda to avoid taxes, or moves a factory to a country where wages are cheaper, it appears that business is unfair. It seeks the benefits of government without paying its share of the burden of government. Taxation is increasingly shifted to individuals. Some of the same issues regarding justice arise here as arose when we considered executive compensation. However, these justice issues have received even less attention.

▲ CONCLUSION ▲

In this chapter we have considered the obligations of managers to non traditional stakeholders – some of whom have not been treated seriously as stakeholders by American business. We have noted that businesses are being held responsible for the activities of their suppliers and that this shift in public perception has important implications for the ethics of supply management. We have also pointed out that the media – especially the investigative media, is an important stakeholder because of its adversarial power and its ability to compete in the public relations game. As a result, the obligations of a manager to the media may be less stringent than is often thought. Namely, nothing more may be required than what is normally required in dealing ethically with traditional competitors. Similar conclusions exist when we consider NGOs – a stakeholder that is already important in other developed countries and thus is already important for American companies that do business in these countries. NGOs are likely to gain importance in the United States as well. Finally, we considered the ethics of relations between business and government. We pointed out that business already receives many benefits from government. We questioned on ethical grounds the tactics of many businesses in gaining advantages from government. However, we also noted that the dynamics of current practice make it extremely difficult for an individual business to behave ethically with respect to lobbying government in its interest. Nonetheless, we noted that if the interests of business and the public interest diverge sufficiently, then a backlash against business may occur. It has happened before and it can happen again.

▲ NOTES ▲

1. This information is found in Ian Maitland's "The Great Non-Debate Over International Sweatshops" in *Ethical Theory and Business*, 7th edition, ed. Tom L. Beauchamp and Norman E. Bowie (Upper Saddle River, NJ: Prentice Hall, 2004), pp. 571–90.
2. Denis G. Arnold, "Human Rights and Global Labor Practices" in *Ethical Theory and Business*, 7th edition, ed. Tom L. Beauchamp and Norman E. Bowie (Upper Saddle River, NJ: Prentice Hall, 2004), p. 563.
3. The detail for this kind of argument can be found in Ian Maitland, "The Great Non-Debate," pp. 587–9.
4. Reported in Denis G. Arnold and Norman E. Bowie, "Sweatshops and Respect for Persons," *Business Ethics Quarterly* 13 (2003), pp. 221–42.
5. Ibid., p. 230.
6. Ibid., p. 231.
7. See Denis Arnold, "Human Rights," p. 566, for a minimalist definition of a living wage provided by the United Nations.
8. See David Card and Alan B. Krueger, *Myth and Measurement: The New Economics of the Minimum Wage* (Princeton, NJ: Princeton University Press, 1995).
9. Quoted in Alex Markels, "Showdown for a Tool in Rights Lawsuits," *New York Times* (June 15, 2003), p. 11.
10. See Aaron Bernstein, "Sweatshops: Finally Airing the Dirty Linen," *Business Week* (June 23, 2003), pp. 100, 102.
11. The information in this paragraph is drawn from Shirley Leung, "McDonalds Wants Suppliers of Meat to Limit Antibiotics Use," *Wall Street Journal* (June 20, 2003), p. B2.
12. Marc Gunther, "Tree Huggers, Soy Lovers and Profits," *Fortune* (June 23, 2003), p. 100.
13. The details of this case can be found in the case written by Kenneth Goodpaster and Anne K. Delehunt, Harvard Business School, cases 9-390-017–9-390-020.
14. For a full defense of this view see John Boatright, "Fiduciary Duties and the Shareholder Management Relation or What's So Special About Shareholders?" *Business Ethics Quarterly* 4 (1994) pp. 393–407.

chapter six

Corporate Social Responsibility

▲ THE COMMUNITY AS STAKEHOLDER ▲

Perhaps the best-known question in business ethics is: Is it morally permissible (morally obligatory) for a company to give away some of its profits for the benefit of the community? Milton Friedman is the best-known source of a negative answer to that question. Friedman's arguments for his position were elaborated in chapter 2. We disagree with Friedman and take the strong position that not only is it permissible for a company to give away some of its profits to the local community but that it has an obligation to do so.

To build an argument for this position, we first need to establish the fact that the local community is a legitimate corporate stakeholder. As you recall, on the narrow definition of stakeholder, the local community would be a stakeholder because the local community is necessary for the survival of the firm. On the negative side, local communities have tremendous power with respect to zoning regulations, the prohibition of certain businesses, and the use of tax policy to let business know if it is welcome or not. On the positive side, the local community provides the infrastructure that makes business possible – fire and police protection, roads, sewers, and highways, and education through grade twelve. The local community is a legitimate stakeholder under the classical definition.

As a legitimate stakeholder, the corporation has duties to the local community just as it receives benefits from the community. A manager can accept the view that the corporation has obligations to the local community without agreeing that these obligations include corporate philanthropy. Managers could argue that they pay taxes and provide jobs and that these activities are sufficient to meet their obligations. Since many companies demand tax breaks and other incentives to locate in a community, the "we pay taxes" argument will not work for many companies. As an aside, it should also be noted that at the national level, a number of corporations have incorporated offshore in places such as Bermuda specifically to avoid the payment of US taxes. Even the "we provide jobs" argument is less persuasive as companies move more of their manufacturing and service operations overseas in order to save labor costs. The process is sometimes referred to as the hollowing out of the corporation.

Corporations can respond, of course, by saying that whatever taxes they pay and regardless of how many they employ, the fact that they employ some and pay some taxes is a positive compared to what would happen if they were not in the local community at all. That is not at all clear. It is possible that the company consumes more in public services than it pays in taxes whether directly or indirectly from the people who work there. Also there is no tradition in the United States of quantifying such things as the value of an educated workforce, which is clearly of great benefit to a company. We should abandon the prejudice that privately produced goods like automobiles and computers are good and valuable, but that services like elementary education and police and fire protection paid from taxes are somehow a necessary evil and likely to be wasteful at that. If anything, recent events have shown us that when certain services are in the hands of for-profit organizations, quality of service is an issue. Few argue that the military should be privately managed on a for-profit basis. In addition we think it no accident that after the September 11 terrorist attack, Congress insisted that airport security be a government rather than a for-profit operation. When you look at all this from a different perspective, it is possible to argue that in many cases the local community gives more to the corporation than it gets in return. If that argument could be sustained for any individual corporation, then there is an argument based on reciprocal obligations and fairness for corporate giving back to the local community through corporate philanthropy.

Another argument a manager might use to deny an obligation for corporate charity is based on a long tradition of individual philanthropy. In other words, the corporation has no obligation to be charitable so long as the corporate officers and managers provide individual support to charity. In the early part of the twentieth century, a number of corporate titans, such as Andrew Carnegie and John D. Rockefeller, established huge foundations to give away their wealth. In addition, these corporate giants personally supported major projects such as the building of libraries, churches, concert halls, and universities. It is no accident that there is a Rockefeller University and a Carnegie-Mellon University. Riverside Church in New York City was built largely with Rockefeller money. This tradition continues with the William and Melinda Gates Foundation that will invest billions of dollars to improve health in Africa. Ted Turner has promised a billion dollars for the United Nations.

Corporate personnel give time as well as money. Corporate leadership has stood behind the "United Way" campaigns in most communities and states. Nearly all corporations strongly encourage all employees to give to the United Way. Indeed, in some instances managers have been accused of putting undue pressure on employees both in terms of giving and in the amount to be given. Be that as it may, successful American business persons have felt an obligation to return some of their wealth to society.

What has occurred at the individual level has evolved at the corporate level to the point where we now can speak of a tradition of corporate philanthropy in the United States that we have not seen to the same extent in other industrialized countries. Many corporations have set up corporate foundations or provide support for the community directly, without that support being mediated by an individual's foundation. Many corporations match the charitable contributions of employees. Some corporations give employees time off with pay when the employees do volunteer work in the community. The Minneapolis/St. Paul metropolitan area provides one of the more interesting examples of corporate philanthropy. Corporations may belong to the 1 percent, 2 percent, or 5 percent clubs in which they pledge to donate the appropriate percentage of their pretax profits to charity. The Minneapolis Chamber of Commerce through its Minnesota Keystone Program manages this program. In 1997 there were 253 members, compared to 23 members when the club was founded in 1976.[1] Although many firms in the Twin Cities have reduced their percentage of giving, the percent clubs continue to play an important role in the community. The retailer Target pledges that part of every dollar spent in its stores will be returned to the local community. Whatever the theoretical merits of Friedman's position, the reality is that at most American corporations, corporate philanthropy is a part of the corporate enterprise. Go to the home page of most corporate websites and you will find that a description of corporate giving is not more than a mouse click away. We think managers engaged in philanthropy are normally behaving ethically. Our ethical principle is that managers have an obligation to manage the charitable enterprise prudently and efficiently, as is their responsibility with any other part of the business.

We recognize that we have simultaneously presented a picture of corporate America as heavily involved in corporate philanthropy while at the same time noting that corporations are demanding tax breaks and other perks in order to either establish a presence in a community or to maintain a presence where they already have one. Is the glass half full or half empty? Some recent research has shown that it is more than half empty. More precisely, the communities would be better off if corporations paid their fair share of taxes and avoided asking for other perks. Corporate philanthropy may be good public relations, but what a community really needs is for corporations to pay taxes.

▲ A PRUDENTIAL ARGUMENT ▲

Often the debate between those who hold to Milton Friedman's position and those who defend corporate philanthropy is viewed as a win/lose rather than a win/win proposition. In other words, if it could be shown that consumers reward those corporations with outstanding records in philanthropy, then philanthropy contributes to the bottom line rather than reduces it. Similarly, if it could be shown that employees have higher morale and thus are more productive at companies with a strong reputation in corporate philanthropy, we would have another situation where giving money away actually makes more money for the stockholders. Such evidence would provide a business case for corporate giving. There is some evidence that the business case is a valid one – at least in some instances. One area where doing good and doing well has had some initial success is with spending to improve the environment. Later in this chapter, management's obligations to the environment will be discussed in some detail.

On the other hand, we must admit that the evidence is mixed. Customers have not seen themselves as morally obligated to patronize those companies that are especially ethical. Although, in this book, we emphasize the obligations of managers to corporate stakeholders, we do believe that the non-managerial stakeholders have moral obligations to moral managers and the firms they manage. However, to detail the responsibilities that other stakeholders owe to managers is the subject of another book.

There are a number of corporations, which have viewed supporting the community and profitability to be a win/win situation. One of those is the Marriott Corporation. The Marriott Corporation trained and then hired 6,000 persons on welfare, including some who had been homeless. Why did they do it? Here is what J. W. Marriott said about the program:

> We're getting good employees for the long term but we're also helping these communities. If we don't step up in these inner cities and provide work, they'll never pull out of it. But it makes bottom line sense. If it didn't, we wouldn't do it.[2]

And a *Business Week* feature article on the Marriott program concludes the same:

> But this isn't a story about altruism. Marriott's unusual approach to the low wage dilemma is dictated by corporate self-interest. Helping workers can cut cost and increase productivity. And that goes right to the bottom line.[3]

Many would argue that if business firms commit to supporting the community because it is profitable, then there is nothing ethical about the commitment. However, we should be cautious here. Such a view reflects a certain theory about ethics, specifically the moral philosophy of Immanuel Kant, who argues that if the motive for the action is not pure – that is, done because it is right – then the action is not truly moral even though the action may be a good one. However, other moral theories, such as utilitarianism, would find the action moral if it leads to the best consequences overall. Moreover, as we have argued elsewhere,[4] managers in publicly held firms have a contractual obligation to seek profit. Thus, seeking profit is one of the moral obligations a manager has, and seeking profit in a sustainable way is moral, even if one is a Kantian.

However, we do believe that motives are important and that managers should be motivated by moral considerations. Making a profit is one appropriate moral motive. Wanting to serve the interests of the other corporate stakeholders is also an appropriate moral motive. A manager should not claim that he is trying to serve the interests of other stakeholders when he is really only concerned about profit, and serving another stakeholder is simply a happy accident. To claim credit for something that is not your intention is hypocritical. However, there is nothing wrong and there is everything right with being motivated to serve the interests of employees, for example, and also trying to make a profit.

But how can you tell about the motives of someone? Well, it is often hard to determine someone's motives. But it is not impossible. As former Chief Justice Oliver Wendell Holmes said, "Even a dog knows the difference between being kicked and being tripped over." Sometimes the motives are pretty clear. Let us turn to the Marriott case. If one were to read the entire *Business Week* article, one would find the following:

> Its [Marriott's] employees drive welfare trainees to work, arrange their day care, negotiate with their landlords, bicker with their case workers, buy them clothes, visit them at home, coach them in everything from banking skills to self-respect – and promise those who stick it out full time jobs at Marriott or elsewhere. Even then, trainees often show up late, work slowly, fight with co-workers, and go AWOL for reasons as simple as a torn stocking.[5]

Kant is rightly famous for the burdens of acting out of duty. For many Marriott employees, training those who had been on welfare was burdensome indeed. Is there any doubt that the managers at Marriott were motivated by their desire to help the community as well as by their desire to contribute to the bottom line? Indeed after reading the *Business Week* article, it seems that the motive to help might have been even stronger than the motive to earn a profit.

In this section, we have provided a historical overview of corporate social responsibility in the United States. We have argued that there are good moral and business reasons for supporting the local community. At the very least, a corporation should do its fair share and put into the community as much as it takes out. We reject the argument that if a company makes a profit from its community service, then the morality of its action is somehow morally tainted. On the contrary, managers have an obligation to make business decisions that benefit the various corporate stakeholders. Win/win decisions are of just this kind. However, corporations should not be hypocritical. Managers should be motivated by a genuine desire to help the community in addition to seeing that there may be a financial advantage in doing so. The example of the Marriott Corporation provides an excellent example of a management that is committed to good works as well as to the bottom line.

Despite all that some US managers have done in the realm of corporate social responsibility, European firms have done even more. Indeed there is an entire movement in Europe supported by NGOs and governments, including the European Union, devoted to a comprehensive plan of corporate social responsibility. We now turn our attention to that movement.

▲ CORPORATE SOCIAL RESPONSIBILITY ▲ (CSR) – EUROPEAN STYLE

In the United States, the emphasis has been on individual and corporate philanthropy and community service. However, a coherent well worked out philosophy of corporate social responsibility has not existed – at least in any way to the same extent – as it does in Europe. The focus of the European CSR movement is the concept of "sustainability." There is also a revolutionary movement afoot to change how one measures a corporation's "success" or profit. Triple bottom-line accounting, as it is called, measures financial success or profits, contributions to a livable environment, and contributions to solving social problems. A manager who can make positive contributions in all three areas manages a sustainable corporation.

We begin our discussion of CSR by examining the official publication on that subject by the European Union. The definition of CSR was developed for the Green Paper released in July 2001. It defines CSR as "a concept whereby companies integrate social and environmental concerns in their business operations and in their interaction with their stakeholders on a voluntary basis." That definition now serves what is called a European Action Framework for CSR. The three main features of CSR that are common throughout Europe are:

1. Behavior over and above the legal requirements, voluntarily adopted because businesses deem it to be in their long-term interest.
2. Behavior linked to the concept of sustainable development.
3. Behavior that is not an optional "add-on" to core business activities but is descriptive of the way business is managed.

The European Commission has developed a strategy for promoting CSR in Europe. The strategy includes:

1. Increasing knowledge about the positive impact of CSR on business and societies in Europe and abroad, particularly in the developing countries.
2. Exchanging information on best practices.
3. Promoting the development of CSR management skills.
4. Fostering CSR among small and mid-size enterprises (SMEs).
5. Facilitating convergence and transparency of CSR practices and tools.
6. Launching a multi-stakeholder forum on CSR at the EU level.
7. Integrating CSR into European Community policies.

As indicated, the focus concept here is sustainability. The concept comes originally from a UN report that defines sustainability as the ability "to meet the needs of the present without compromising the ability of future generations to meet their own needs."[6] The so-called three pillars of sustainability are successful financial, environmental, and social results. In addition to being financially successful, a sustainable business is one that addresses the genuine needs of people without harming the environment over the long term.

How can managers implement a strategy of sustainable development? Since we have endorsed the stakeholder manager in this text, we recommend that managers initiate stakeholder dialogs. As we noted in chapter 2, a number of companies that are members of CSR Europe now regularly hold stakeholder forums. British Petroleum (BP) and Royal Dutch Shell (Shell) do extensive and regular stakeholder dialogs. Both BP and Shell are involved in major oil and gas exploration efforts and in the building of pipelines.

Let us examine the philosophy of both companies and then see how it is being implemented in the countries where the pipeline is being built. A visit to BP's website gives you the following:

Policy:
Within any broad group of stakeholders there will always be conflicting interests and a lack of consensus on issues. Although this is the case, we believe that understanding the aspirations and concerns of our stakeholders is essential for our continued business success. Without this knowledge, we cannot be fully aware of the risks and opportunities that our business activity faces, and the potential impact that our stakeholders can have on our plans.

Working With Stakeholders:
Stakeholder engagements can take many forms in BP but generally
they fall into three categories:
ongoing direct contact on a formal or informal basis
indirect feedback mediated by a third party
structured debates with special interest groups.

How is the policy implemented? BP is building a major pipeline
from the Caspian Sea to the Mediterranean. The pipeline will by-pass
the heavily navigated and dangerous Bosporus Strait. Among the
countries that the pipeline will cross are Azerbaijan, Georgia, and
Turkey: BP, which has a policy of stakeholder engagement, has
carried on extensive stakeholder engagements in all countries that the
pipeline transverses. One of the more creative stakeholder dialogs was
women-only dialogs in Turkey, where women would receive an
update on the pipeline project and be given the opportunity to ask
questions. The women's concerns centered on security, pollution,
safety and health, and the impact of the project on agriculture and
infrastructure. British Petroleum issues a special report, "Environmental and Social Review," each year. This review is audited for
accuracy. Ernst and Young audited the 2002 report. A visit to the BP
website will provide accounts of numerous stakeholder engagements
in various parts of the world – Angola and China, for example.

Perhaps the company that best embodies the European ideal of
sustainable business is Royal Dutch Shell, the eighth largest company
in terms of sales in the world. As we previously noted, Shell had been
criticized by environmentalists for its handling of the *Brent Spar* and
for its failure in Nigeria to try to save the life of dissident Ken Saro-
Wiwa. Both of these events had been written up in Harvard Business
School cases. Shell decided that it had to change its corporate culture
so that it could better manage these non-business factors. Shell has
now endorsed stakeholder management and sustainability. It has
changed its policy regarding non-intervention in political affairs. Its
2002 annual report of the Shell Petroleum Development Company of
Nigeria is divided into three main sections that correspond to the
categories found in triple bottom-line accounting. These are
economic performance, community development performance, and
environmental and safety performance. (By the way, despite the acute
embarrassment over overstated oil reserves in early 2004, we urge the
reader to visit Shell's website. It is a treasure trove of information on
Shell's commitment to sustainability.)

Although Europe is the clear leader in discussions of sustainability, American firms are involved. One can see this by going to the website of CSR Europe and discover that many American companies are members. Given the lack of emphasis on CSR and sustainability in the US, an American reader will be surprised to see the number of American companies that are members of CSR Europe. The list includes Levis, IBM, Johnson & Johnson, Coca-Cola, Ford, GM, Mattel, Microsoft, Motorola, Citigroup, Proctor and Gamble, Hewlett Packard, McDonald's, and Dow.[7]

Finally, it should be noted that around the world there are efforts to encourage sustainable management practices that are committed to specific normative principles. The most ambitious project is the Draft Norms of Responsibilities of Transnational Corporations and Other Business Enterprises with Regard to Human Rights. Another international effort affiliated with the UN Global Social Compact is the Global Reporting Initiative. It is designed to provide a common framework for reporting on the three key elements of sustainability – the economic, the environmental, and the social. There are many American companies that are participating in the project, including such household names as Johnson & Johnson, Ford, Hewlett Packard, McDonald's, Nike, Procter and Gamble, Intel, and 3M. Although American multinationals do not emphasize their participation in such organizations as CSR Europe and the Global Reporting Initiative, given the lack of interest in the US, they nonetheless realize that in the international arena a commitment to sustainability is a competitive requirement.

It should be noted that participating companies believe there is a business case to be made for sustainability. These companies simply believe that sustainable management practices are essential to their long-range survival. Indeed, in this highly competitive world of international business where sustainability is not universally practiced, if the business case cannot be made, sustainability will be nothing more than a passing fad.

▲ MANAGEMENT'S OBLIGATION ▲ TO THE ENVIRONMENT

A useful way of characterizing a manager's obligations to the environment is to look at an increasingly stringent set of obligations.

These obligations have been characterized as legal green, market green, stakeholder green, and dark green.[8]

The first obligation is an easy one: Managers have a duty to obey environmental laws. This is legal green and is taken as a given. Managers have an obligation to obey the law and laws protecting the environment are no exception. A somewhat more complicated issue is whether management does anything wrong when it lobbies against environmental laws.

The second obligation is also an easy one: Managers have a duty to take any step that would both increase profits and improve the environment. This is market green. The Dupont Company was one of the earlier leaders in showing the vast savings that could be made by eliminating waste and recycling. More recently Dupont has tried to transform itself into a dark green company. Many of the *Fortune* 500 companies have recognized the business case for market green and have begun to act accordingly. In addition, the reader may have noticed some changes in America's hospitality industry that have been borrowed from Europe and Asia. For example, hotels change the bed linens for a multiple night stay only if you ask. Also, if you leave your towels on the rack they will not be changed. In a few hotels, when you take your room key and leave the room, the lights automatically go out. In Europe, escalators do not run unless people approach them. Perhaps that will be the next thing we import. However, many small and medium-size enterprises (SMEs) have not moved as far to capture the economic benefits from environmentally friendly actions.

The third obligation requires that managers "create and sustain competitive advantage by responding to the environmental preferences of stakeholders." Fulfilling this obligation might mean that a manufacturer would need to manage the supply chain so that suppliers would meet green requirements – for example, by making their products recyclable. Recall the McDonald's example from chapter 5. Stakeholder green might also require that employees be educated about environmental issues, and it might also require that companies give employees time off to participate in community efforts to improve the environment. The manager should also reach out to those members of the investment community who wish to support green companies. What is required here is that managers look toward the environmentally concerned members of each stakeholder group and manage toward their interests.

This strategy could be much more demanding than the other two. Whereas legal green and market green enable a manager to align the company's interest and environmental interest, stakeholder green may not always be able to present a win/win situation. Suppose most of its customers are not concerned about the environment, especially if the quality or convenience of the product were to be affected. If the majority of any stakeholder group were not particularly green, then profits really could diminish – especially in the short term. If the manager were to give priority to stakeholder members who are environmentally conscious, especially if they are a small minority of the stakeholder group, then profits could certainly be adversely affected.

In the United States, this is not as far-fetched as one might think. Americans think they have a natural right to low gas prices and have a love affair with the SUV. Our top-loading washing machines are neither efficient at washing clothes nor energy efficient. Americans will not adopt the smaller front-loading washing machines that are common in the rest of the world. The restaurant chain Wendy's tried to replace foam plates and cups with paper ones, but customers in the test market balked. Procter and Gamble offered Downey fabric softener in concentrated form that requires less packaging than ready-to-use products; however, the concentrate version is less convenient because it has to be mixed with water – sales have been poor. Proctor and Gamble manufactures Vizur and Lenor brands of detergent in concentrate form, which the customer mixes at home in reusable bottles. Europeans will take the trouble; Americans will not. Kodak tried to eliminate its yellow film boxes but met with customer resistance. McDonald's has been testing mini-incinerators that convert trash into energy, but often meets opposition from community groups that fear the incinerators will pollute the air. A McDonald's spokesperson points out that the emissions are mostly carbon dioxide and water vapor and "are less offensive than a barbecue." [9]

The reluctance of the consumer to practice "green" presents a dilemma for the manager. The manager might try to absolve him- or herself of all responsibility and simply follow the dictates of the market. But that would not be stakeholder green management. Managers have an obligation to educate their customers, and in some cases it is not difficult to do. Once the hotels point out that there is an option not to change the sheets every day, many of us have opted not to have them changed. After all, we do not change the sheets on our bed at home every day. We believe managers have an obligation to educate consumers to practice green, especially when their doing so will contribute to bottom-line results.

The final and most demanding strategy has to be dark green. Dark green companies are committed to being leaders in respecting the environment. Dark green managers manage according to the following principle: "Create and sustain value in a way that sustains and cares for the earth."[10] Some companies do aspire to be dark green and, surprisingly, some are in industries that have dismal environmental records – chemicals and oil, for example. One of the most committed companies is Dupont.[11] Dupont CEO Charles O. Holliday Jr. wrote a book on corporate social responsibility entitled *Walking the Talk: The Business Case for Sustainability*. One of Dupont's goals is "to own a collection of businesses that can go on forever without depleting natural resources."[12] By 2010 Dupont wants to generate 25 percent of its resources from renewables. Tyvek, a Dupont insulation product, saves more energy than it requires to produce it. The acquisition of Pioneer Hi-Bred International enabled Dupont to turn corn into stretch shirts.

Another leader is Interface Corporation.[13] The carpet-making industry is another industry that has considered to be especially hard on the environment. Most carpet fibers are made from a non-renewable resource, petroleum. The waste produced in carpet manufacturing contains toxins and heavy metals and produces CO_2 emissions. CO_2 is widely believed to be associated with global warming. Carpet is generally not recycled and ends up in landfills where it sits, toxic and non-biodegradable.

Interface has turned the assumptions about carpet manufacturing on their head. Rather than sell carpeting, Interface leases it. Now the incentives shift so that there are incentives to either long-lasting carpet or recyclable carpet. They also manufacture carpeting that can be easily replaced in sections. In making this shift, Interface has become more efficient and reduced energy and material costs significantly. The leadership of Interface shows that the carpet industry need not be the environmental menace it has been in the past.

One of the strategies suggested throughout this book for ethical management is the use of stakeholder dialogs. We should note that stakeholder dialog in the environmental area could be especially difficult because some environmental advocates have metaphysical and moral views that will be unfamiliar to most managers. For example, we normally speak of moral obligations to individuals or collections of individuals. However, some environmentalists who are deep ecologists speak of our obligations to the environment per se.

The classic expression of this view is from Aldo Leopold in *A Sand County Almanac*. "A thing is right when it tends to preserve the integrity, stability, and beauty of the bionic community. It is wrong when it tends to do otherwise."[14] At the metaphysical level, deep ecologists tend to be holists about the environment. That is, they see the total environment as having a reality over and above the individuals that make it up. Looking at the environment in this way, they believe, better enables them to see the interconnections that exist within the environment. They try to look at the environment as a whole. In this way they give the environment as a whole greater ethical status than the objects that make it up. Theoretically, a deep ecologist could sacrifice human beings for the benefit of the planet as a whole. Less radically, a deep ecologist would favor limits on human population and on ever increasing human consumption. This perspective will not fit well with the ideas of most people – especially most managers – who look at protecting the environment as a matter of protecting it for us humans and not as a matter of protecting the environment per se. Genuine stakeholder dialog with deep ecologists about the environment may be impossible, but perhaps the effort should be made. However, if the effort is to be made, a manager must be committed to the philosophy of dark green. No lighter shade of green will do.

As we indicated earlier, Shell is one company that recognizes that it needs to have a dialog even with those with whom it most strenuously disagrees, and this is a company that knows its business strategy will need to evolve to accommodate the diverse pressures that result from being in the energy business. The following "ad" from Shell appeared in the September 1, 2003, *Economist*:

> We're all involved in the oil business. Every time we start our cars, turn on our lights, cook a meal or heat our homes, we're relying on some form of fuel to make it happen. Up to now, it's inevitably been a fossil fuel, part of the carbon chain. And, just as inevitably, that will have to change. Long before we decide to stop using fossil fuels, costs will have already made the difference for us. Not just the monetary cost, but the human cost, the cultural cost, the environmental cost. We will, quite rightly, demand that our future energy is both sustainable and renewable. We will expect a lot from the likes of solar power, wind power, geothermal power, and hydrogen fuel cells. And it will take time.
>
> Various estimates suggest that by 2050, nearly one third of the world's energy needs could come from these resources. Which leaves

the other two thirds to come from conventional fuels such as oil and gas. To make that happen we will have to strike a balance. Between the need to protect people's way of life and their environment and the need to provide them with affordable energy. Between the cost of developing new technology to extract the utmost from current fuels and the cost of developing new power sources. This is what Shell does every day all over the world. This is why we need to hear from and listen to, everyone who has an interest in the world. Which is pretty much everyone in the world. This is the real price of energy and it's worth it, if only to make sure that our children have a chance to buy it. And a world worth buying it in.

A platform for all points of view is at www.shell.com.

But is there any real hope that stakeholder dialog with ecologists who hold such different views can really reach a consensus on policy and action? Remarkably there is some hope. The environmental philosopher Bryan Norton has shown that despite differences in philosophy there is considerable consensus on action.[15] For example, there is widespread consensus that biological diversity ought to be preserved. Joseph Desjardins has suggested four areas where there is already considerable agreement, In addition to the preservation of biological diversity, he cites waste and pollution, the use of natural resources, and the preservation of environmentally sensitive areas.[16] However, the consensus that Desjardins points out is very limited in nature. For example, there is agreement that where possible pollution should be eliminated, if possible we should use renewable resources rather than non-renewable ones, that some areas should be protected from development, and there are prudent reasons for promoting biological diversity.[17] Agreed, but the devil is in the details. The alleged consensus requires tradeoffs and it is with the tradeoffs that disagreement lies. Desjardins also identifies specific obligations for managers with respect to the environment. Business has the obligation to dramatically increase the productivity of natural resources (ecoefficiency). We agree, since this requirement is consistent with being market green. Desjardins also contends that managers have an obligation to integrate former wastes back into the production system or to transform wastes into biologically beneficial elements, or minimally not to produce wastes faster than the biosphere can absorb them. In many cases this obligation is consistent with both market green and stakeholder green. However, there are certainly times when that is not the case. To ensure a level playing field in this respect, legislation would be required. The same is true when we consider Desjardins' third requirement: Managers have an obligation to "not use resources at rates faster than what can be replenished by the biosphere, and especially ought not to destroy the productive capacity of the biosphere itself." Although we believe these are noble goals, we also believe that real progress will require the kind of stakeholder dialog that we have advocated throughout this book.

▲ CONCLUSION ▲

Whatever the merits of the philosophical discussion, it seems as if business executives and managers in the US have accepted the notion of corporate philanthropy as well as the notion of individual philanthropy. Many managers who do so believe there is a business case to be made for corporate philanthropy. When that is true, a manager can both fulfill his or her obligations to the stockholders and those to other stakeholders. Despite the rhetoric of stakeholder management in the US, there is considerable skepticism and indeed cynicism about stakeholder management. Significantly, European managers seem to take the notion of corporate social responsibility more seriously because they have implemented it into their daily business operations. Through the use of triple bottom-line accounting they have tried to measure firms' progress in being socially responsible or – as they would say – in running a sustainable business. We urge American business firms to move to the next level – to move from corporate philanthropy to corporate social responsibility through the running of a sustainable business. Only then will a manager's obligations to the community be fully met.

▲ NOTES ▲

1. Wilfred Bockelman, *Culture of Corporate Citizenship* (Lakeville, MN: Galde Press, 2000), p. 81.
2. Dana Milbank, "Hiring Welfare Workers, Hotel Chain Finds It Tough But Rewarding," *Wall Street Journal* (October 31, 1996), p. A1.
3. Catherine Young, "Low Wage Lessons," *Business Week* (November 11, 1996), p. 116.
4. Bowie, *Business Ethics: A Kantian Perspective* (Malden, MA: Blackwell, 1999), p. 139.
5. Ibid., p. 140.

6. Joseph Desjardins, *Business Ethics* (Englewood Cliffs, NJ: McGraw Hill, 2003), p. 175.
7. http://www.csreurope.org/membership/default.asp?pageid = 385.
8. These terms are from R. Edward Freeman, Jessica Pierce, and Richard Dodd, "Shades of Green: Business Ethics and the Environment," reprinted in *Ethical Theory and Business*, 6th edition, ed. Tom L. Beauchamp and Norman E. Bowie (Upper Saddle River, NJ: Prentice Hall, 2001), pp. 216–23.
9. Alicia Swasy, "For Consumers, Ecology Comes Second," *Wall Street Journal* (August 23, 1988), p. B1.
10. Freeman *et al.*, "Shades of Green," p. 222.
11. The information on DuPont is from Marc Gunther, "Tree Huggers, Soy Lovers, and Profits," *Fortune* (June 23, 2003), pp. 98–104.
12. Ibid., p. 99.
13. This account is taken from Desjardins, *Business Ethics*, pp. 174–6 and 194–5.
14. Aldo Leopold, *A Sand County Almanac* (New York: Oxford University Press, 1949), p. 262.
15. Bryan Norton, *Towards Unity Among Environmentalists* (New York: Oxford University Press, 1991).
16. Desjardins, *Business Ethics*, p. 179.
17. Ibid., pp. 180–1.

chapter seven

Moral Imagination, Stakeholder Theory, and Systems Thinking: One Approach to Management Decision-making[1]

Written with Patricia H. Werhane

ExxonMobil is a new company formed by the merger of Exxon and Mobil, two oil companies that have been in business for almost a century. Two years ago, in partnership with ChevronTexaco and Petronas (a Malaysian company), the newly formed company considered investing $3.5 billion in oil drilling in Chad and in building a 600-mile pipeline through Cameroon. The project would generate over a billion barrels of oil, $5.7 billion in revenues for ExxonMobil, $2 billion in revenues for Chad, and $500 million for Cameroon over the 25-year projected drilling period. The project would be a challenging one and had attracted a great deal of world attention.

Chad and Cameroon are two of the poorest countries in the world. Per capita income in each country is less than $1/day. As a comparison, ExxonMobil's 2001 revenues were $190 billion; Chad's GDP was $1.4 billion. According to Transparency International (TI), Chad and Cameroon are also two countries with very poor records for corruption, and they repeatedly come out near the bottom of TI's corruption list, which it publishes every year.[2] The pipeline would go through Cameroon's rain forest, an ecologically fragile but important environmental outpost in Africa. Several tribes of Pygmies and Bantu, whose lifestyle depends on forest products, inhabit that forest.

Originally the Chad–Cameroon project was to be a joint venture including Shell, TotalFinaElf, and ExxonMobil. However, Shell and TotalFinaElf pulled out. According to sources close to these companies, Shell feared another Ogoniland, its often-sabotaged oil fields in southeast Nigeria. Ogoniland proved to be Shell's nemesis for environmental, social, cultural, and political reasons. This project had generated years of alleged environmental and social degradation and very bad press for Shell.[3]

Shell, like many oil companies drilling in remote areas or in less developed countries, had approached the Ogoniland project using their standard operating procedures for oil drilling, an approach, as Shell now admits, that was a simple one, too simple. This is an over-exaggeration, but sometimes in the past the oil-drilling philosophy was to apply almost identical drilling processes in every site all around the world. One found prospects for oil, got government permission to drill, brought in drilling equipment and foreign drilling experts, hired a few local people for more menial temporary jobs, drilled, laid pipeline, pumped out oil, and paid royalties to the government in question. More enlightened companies took into account the local communities that were affected by the drilling (building a school or hospital), and of late, the pipes themselves have been improved to minimize spills, which, even under the best conditions account for 2–3 percent loss of oil every year at every site. Still, at least according to protesters living in Ogoniland, local conditions, culture, governmental structures or the lack thereof (except when sensitive payments were required), environmental issues, and the long-term effects of these projects on the people, the area, and the country were not always taken into account in a serious way from the perspective of those living in oil-drilling areas.

ExxonMobil had been economically successful in drilling in less developed countries (LDCs) in the past. Why should the company change its modus operandi? However, the history of Shell in Ogoniland, Mobil's alleged payoffs to government officials in Kazakhstan,[4] and Exxon's *Valdez* disaster were reason enough for a company to rethink its approach to new drilling in LDCs with reputations and environmental challenges of the kind in Chad and Cameroon.[5] The Chad/Cameroon project presented a challenge, not to its expertise at drilling, but to thinking about how to expedite this venture while avoiding problems of previous explorations. To do this would require that ExxonMobil rethink its traditional exploration models and that it revise its "standard operating procedures" or traditional mental models for oil exploration that have worked well in developed countries. In other words, Exxon Mobil needed to develop moral imagination.

This case, as we have described it, illustrates what is at issue in this chapter: The challenge of managers, executives, and companies to think creatively while at the same time avoiding moral morasses, particularly when doing business such as oil exploration in unfamiliar cultural, social, and political territories. The replicability of standardized operating practices, so easily accomplished in industrial countries, is always at issue, particularly in less developed regions. How one develops methods to think "out of the box" is critical for the economic and moral success of these projects. Why is it that this is so hard, and why is it that so many companies faltered in enterprises with which they have expertise? How does one become morally imaginative when drilling in an area of the world that is poor, remote, corrupt, and culturally alien? The short answer is, only with great difficulty and with tremendous moral risk. These are the issues we shall explore in this chapter.

▲ MINDSETS AND MENTAL MODELS ▲

The idea of moral imagination originates from the very simple but controversial contention that human beings deal with the world through, and only through, socially constructed mindsets or mental models. That idea probably originated with the eighteenth-century philosopher, Immanuel Kant. Kant questioned the standard view of his era that our minds are merely receptacles, either filled with innate ideas we inherit at birth, or blank tablets that are "written on" with whatever experiences we have during our lives. It was Kant who perhaps first questioned both views. Kant noticed that the content of our experiences depends on what we encounter. But the ways in which experiences are organized and ordered are not themselves experienced. For example, we experience all phenomena in space and through time, but neither space nor time are themselves experienced. So, Kant concluded, the structure of experiences, the ways in which they are formulated and ordered, since they are not themselves experienced, must come from our minds. That is, our minds are constitutive of our experiences such that categories or principles of the understanding order and organize the data of what we encounter, phenomena, into what we call experiences.[6]

Many contemporary philosophers debate whether our minds are "hard-wired" as Kant envisioned. Nevertheless, it is commonly (although not universally) concluded that human beings deal with the world through, and indeed only through, socially constructed mindsets or mental models such that, as Peter Railton said, "our conceptual scheme[s] mediate even our most basic perceptual experiences."[7] Mental representations, or cognitive frames, set up parameters though which all experience, or sets of experiences, are organized or filtered. We cannot get at the world, at the so-called external world, except through these formulations, frames, and redescriptions.[8]

Another way to think of this is to argue that we formulate movies of the world. That is, each of us is in a sense a director, filming the world through our own mindset, selecting, editing, deleting, and even distorting what we experience. These forms of sense-making are socially learned, just as making movies is, and they are changeable. Each mindset or mental model limits the scope, scale, and focus of what we experience, and what is included or left out creates frames that can also be evaluated, if only from another circumscribed perspective.[9] These mental models function, too, as formulae not only to replicate our experiences but also, if they work well, as models or exemplars.

Mental models might be hypothetical constructs of the experience in question or scientific theories, or they might be schema that frame the experience, through which individuals process information, conduct experiments, and formulate theories. Mental models function as selective mechanisms and filters for dealing with experience. In focusing, framing, organizing, and ordering what we experience, mental models bracket and leave out data, and emotional and motivational foci taint or color experience. Nevertheless, because schema we employ are socially learned and altered through religion, socialization, culture, educational upbringing, and other experiences, they are shared ways of perceiving, organizing, and learning.

Because of the variety and diversity of mental models, none is complete, and "there are multiple possible framings of any given situation."[10] By that we mean that each of us can frame any situation, event, or phenomenon in more than one way, and that the same phenomenon can also be socially constructed in a variety of ways. It will turn out that the way one frames a situation is critical to its outcome, because "[t]here are different ... moral consequences depending on the way we frame the situation."[11]

▲ MORAL IMAGINATION ▲

Werhane defines moral imagination as:

> the ability in particular circumstances to discover and evaluate
> possibilities not merely determined by that circumstance, or limited
> by its operative mental models, or merely framed by a set of rules or
> rule-governed concerns.[12]

The notion of moral imagination is by and large a facilitating
reasoning process that helps us out of a particular framing box,
leading us to refocus our attention, critique, revise, and reconstruct
other operative mental models, and to develop more creative
normative perspectives. Moral imagination begins with the
particular – a particular person, an event, a situation, a dilemma,
or a conflict. It also requires the ability to disengage – to step back
from the situation and take another perspective, or at least, to be able
to begin a critical evaluation of the situation and its operative mental
models. Part of being *morally* imaginative is to perceive the ethical
dimensions of a managerial or corporate situation and its operative
mindsets, activities that are possible only when one disengages or
steps back from the situation. Of course, if it is true that we deal
with the world only through socially constructed mindsets, no one
can ever disengage themselves completely or take a "view from
nowhere." Our revisions, critiques, and evaluations are still context-
driven by history, circumstances, culture, education, and personal
framing choices. However, just as children playact, so too we can
devise ways to disengage and step back to examine ourselves and our
projects from a somewhat disinterested or distanced perspective.

Unlike other forms of imagination, moral imagination deals not
with fantasies, but with possibilities that, if not practical, are at least
theoretically viable and actualizable. Further, because we are talking
here of *moral* imagination, these possibilities have a normative or
prescriptive character; they concern what one ought to do, with right
and wrong, with virtue, with positive or negative outcomes, or with
what common morality calls "good" or "evil." That is, these
judgments involve principle-based reasoning.

Moral imagination involves not only perceiving ethical nuances,
disengagement from the situation at hand, and fantasizing creatively
about fresh opportunities or new possibilities from a normative
perspective. It is not mere "second guessing." It also should entail

work at developing fresh solutions based on revised or even different mental models. Finally, being morally imaginative requires that one evaluates new possibilities or solutions from a normative perspective, judging not only the possibilities but also the mindsets in which such possibilities are operative.

In summary, being morally imaginative includes:

- Self-reflection about oneself and one's situation, perhaps taking the point of view of another.
- Disengagement from and becoming aware of one's situation, understanding the mental model or script dominating that situation, and envisioning possible moral conflicts or dilemmas that might arise in that context or as outcomes of the dominating scheme.
- The ability to imagine reformulated or even new possibilities. These possibilities include those that are not merely context-dependent and that might involve another set, albeit overlapping mental models, within the range possible given one's situation.
- Moral evaluation both of the original context and its dominating mental models, and the alternatives one has envisioned.[13]

Let us illustrate moral imagination at work. The Bank of Bangladesh has, until recently, controlled the inflow of money into that country and the kinds of loans available to Bangladeshis. Taking a lead from sound Western financial education and advice from the IMF and the World Bank, the bank lends money only to those who have good credit ratings, collateral, or other demonstrated assurances that the loan will either be paid back or can be collected in some fashion. Moreover, because Bangladesh is a Muslim country where paying interest is considered usury and wrong, funding must be couched in complex terminology so as not (at least theoretically) to involve interest payments. All of this seems sensible to the Western mind. However, because most of the population of Bangladesh has no money or collateral, and poor education, they have no ability to borrow money through these conventional sources. The population is too large and the country is too poor to instigate a welfare system. So the poor and the poorest of the poor remained so because of the financial requirements of the system.

However, since 1976 there has been a dramatic change in Bangladesh. Upon returning to his country after studying in the United States, a Muslim Bangladeshi, Muhammad Yunus, was struck with the realization that his country received a great deal of foreign aid, yet most of his people remained in abject poverty. He and his students discovered that part of the problem, in a country with high unemployment and little opportunity for job creation, was the inability of those without capital and property to borrow enough money to develop entrepreneurial enterprises and thus work out of poverty. That is, the prevailing banking mindset, one developed extensively from Western thinking, was that sound financial institutions cannot lend money to people without collateral. So, except for loans available at up to 200 percent from fairly questionable sources, there were no resources available for the poor in Bangladesh. Seeing the need for low-interest rate loans, Yunus scraped the mindset he had learned in graduate school at Vanderbilt University and began to question the religious restrictions on lending. He then formed the Grameen Bank with the philosophy of lending money *only* to those without capital or property, the exact inverse of traditional banking philosophy. Today the Grameen Bank serves over 40,000 villages, and the bank has over 2 million members/borrowers, 97 percent of whom are women. Despite criticism from religious leaders, it lends about $40 to $60 million a month, and its rate of loan loss is under 2 percent. The bank has subsequently expanded into other industries, developed a cell-phone service in rural communities, and is planning training and job development in the new economy of wireless networking and Internet services in a number of rural communities. Almost half of the Grameen members are now economically above the poverty line, mortality rates have been drastically reduced, and 37 percent of children of Grameen members complete primary education. In this process, Yunus has revolted against both traditional banking practices and the systemic subjugation of women in his country. This was enormously risky both financially and morally; yet he has succeeded and set a model for micro lending that is now being copied in at least 65 other underdeveloped countries around the world.[14]

Cynics might argue that Yunus was merely seizing an entrepreneurial opportunity and has found a new way to make money. This may be true, because the Grameen Bank has never lost money since its inception. However, it has also never been enormously profitable, and all its income is put back into new development projects.

▲ MORAL IMAGINATION AND SYSTEMS ▲ THINKING

So far we have approached the notion of moral imagination primarily from the individualistic perspective of a single decision-maker. However, this belies all of what is at stake. Yunus, for example, while initially working alone, had to work within the cultural context of his country and take those restraints into account. While it is true that he managed to overcome what to his mind was shortsightedness in Bangladeshi banking, he could not ignore the context, culture, and religious restraints of the country completely. Moreover, he needed Western banking knowledge as the starting point for developing a micro lending mindset, which he created. Similarly, in the example with which we began this chapter, ExxonMobil's projected oil exploration in Chad and Cameroon involved a complex network of relationships embedded in a complex set of systems and subsystems, including the cultures of two countries and their diverse indigenous populations, environmental issues, financing, pressures from non-governmental organizations (NGOs), and, it will turn out, the World Bank. To deal with ethical issues in these and other cases either from an individual or even from an organizational perspective, may oversimplify what is really at issue and thus ignore a number of important elements. To evaluate these cases and to develop rich decision-making skills may require what the organizational and scientific literature calls "systems thinking" or a systems approach.

What do we mean by "systems thinking" or a "systems approach?" Systems thinking has different definitions, depending on the discipline. For our purposes, systems thinking presupposes that most of our thinking, experiencing, practices, and institutions are interrelated and interconnected. Almost everything we can experience or think about is in a network of interrelationships such that each element of a particular set of interrelationships affects the other components of that set and the system itself. Almost no phenomenon can be studied in isolation from all relationships with at least some other phenomena.

Systems thinking, then, involves two kinds of analysis. In a systems approach, "concentration is on the analysis and design of the whole, as distinct from . . . the components or parts."[15] Systems thinking requires conceiving of the system as a whole with interdependent elements, subsystems, and networks of relationships and patterns of interaction. Studying a particular component of a system or a particular relationship is valuable only if one recognizes that that study is an abstraction from a more systemic consideration.

Second, few systems are merely linear and few are closed systems that are not constantly in dynamic processes of changing and reinventing themselves. Therefore, systems thinking involves multiple-perspective analyses of any subject matter.[16] So each system or subsystem, because it is complex and entails a multitude of various individual, empirical, social, and political relationships, needs to be analyzed from multiple perspectives.

Mitroff and Linstone postulate that any phenomenon, organization, or system should be dealt with from at least three perspectives, each of which involves different worldviews in which each challenges the others in dynamic exchanges of questions and ideas. Mitroff and Linstone suggest that in business, economic, and public policy contexts one needs to look at problems from a technical or fact-finding point of view, from an organizational or social relationships perspective, and from an individual perspective, ranking problems, perspectives, and alternate solutions, and evaluating the problem and its possible resolution from these multiple perspectives.[17]

A multiple perspectives approach also takes into account the fact that each of us individually, or as groups, organizations, or systems, creates and frames the world through a series of mental models, each of which, by itself, is incomplete. It is impossible to take account of all the networks of relationships involved in a particular system, especially since these systems interact over time. Nevertheless, a multiple perspectives approach forces us to think more broadly, and to look at particular systems or problems from different points of view. This is crucial in trying to avoid problems such as might be encountered by ExxonMobil in their new project, because each perspective usually "reveals insights ... that are not obtainable in principle from others."[18] It is also invaluable in trying to understand other points of view, even if, eventually, one makes decisions that adversely affect others.

▲ THE SYSTEMS APPROACH AND ▲ STAKEHOLDER THEORY

In examining ethical issues in systems, subsystems, and organizations, one way to think about a multiple perspectives approach is to develop an overlapping set of two grids, the elements of which we shall initially label descriptive and normative. We shall see, however, that these are provisional labels, because the two elements overlap considerably.

The first, a descriptive or "technical" approach, includes the following. First one describes the system in question from a sociological point of view. Included in the description are networks of interrelationships between individuals, groups, organizations, and systems, and the number, nature, and scope of subsystems in the system in question. One outlines the boundaries and boundary-creating activities so that it is clear what is not included in the system. Stakeholder theory is useful in this context. By enumerating the various stakeholders involved in or affected by the system, their interrelationships and accountabilities, one can become clearer on the networks of interrelationships entailed in a particular system.[19]

Linked to the boundary conditions and stakeholder prioritization are the accountability relationships between each stakeholder and element of the system in question. Being clear about these relationships, and how each individual and each element of the system is or should be accountable to each other, helps to clarify where decisions go wrong. It is tempting to conceive those dyadically, as Figure 7.1 illustrates. And from an organizational approach a dyadic description of accountability may be adequate. But as our two cases illustrate, organizations are parts of more complex systems, and

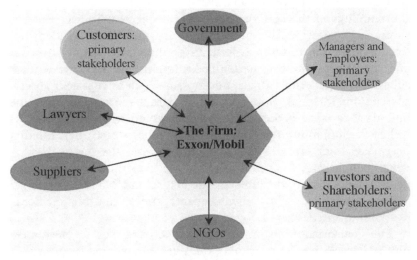

Figure 7.1 Standard stakeholder "map."

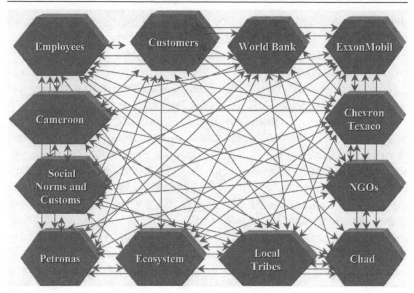

Figure 7.2 ExxonMobil Stakeholder Networks.

these relationships are much more overlapping and interlocking. See Figure 7.2 for a partial graphic depiction of some of these.

However, this is not enough. Different stakeholders will outline the boundary conditions differently because of the way they prioritize what is important – their values. Thus the descriptive grid imports normative/evaluative components in evaluating the shortcomings of the boundary perceptions, accountability relationships, and goal prioritization. But there are other elements a normative dimension introduces as well. From the normative perspective, one investigates how a particular configuration of a system or subsystem affects individuals, micro issues such as customer access, shareholder interests, and political constraints. One evaluates the boundary-creating processes to be clear about what is left out, as well as accountability relationships, as we illustrated earlier. Finally, one needs to determine what goals or purposes the system has, or what goals it *should* have, and how these are prioritized, since the goals a system has will affect its structure and interrelationships. These prioritized goals then become the evaluative elements overlaid on the descriptive grid.

The goal-orientation of any system accounts for its normative dimensions. As has been argued extensively elsewhere, organizations as well as individuals have purposes and goals that carry with them moral obligations, and we hold organizations and institutions, as well as individuals, morally accountable.[20] While it is less transparent that systems are moral agents of some sort, it is true that the structure, interrelationships, and goals of a particular system produce outcomes that have normative consequences. An alteration of a particular system or parts of that system will often produce different kinds of outcomes. Networks of relationships between individuals, groups, and institutional systems are relationships between people. The character and operations of a particular system or set of systems affects those of us who come in contact with the system, whether we are individuals, the community, professionals, managers, companies, or government agencies. Thus, moral responsibility is incurred by the nature and characteristics of the system in question.[21] For example, we tend to blame the political economists and banks in Bangladesh for the country's endemic poverty even though there appears to be no one set of individuals we can single out, given what is taken to be sound financial philosophy such that apparently they conclude that there is "nothing they can do about it."

Systemic arrangements and organizational networks create roles and role responsibilities, rights, and opportunities that affect individuals and individual activities and performance. What is less obvious is that one can take a single organization or a single individual functioning within that organization or system and apply different systems' matrices to that organization with differing outcomes. What subsystems and individuals functioning within these systems focus on, and the ways values and stakeholders are prioritized, affects the goals, procedures, and outcomes of the system or subsystem in question. On every level, the way we frame the goals, the procedures, and what networks we take into account makes a difference in what we discover and what we neglect. These framing mechanisms will turn out to be important normative influences of systems and systems thinking, as we shall illustrate later in returning to the ExxonMobil case.

▲ SYSTEMS THINKING, BOUNDARY ▲ CONDITIONS, AND MORAL IMAGINATION

We have left underdetermined what we mean by "boundary conditions" and how they are limiting. One way in which they are limiting is because of the operative mental models or mindsets of any particular system, organization, or subsystem. Mental models, as Peter Senge reminds us,[22] function on the organizational and systemic levels as well as in individual cognition. So often we find ourselves within an organizational culture that creates mental habits that function as boundary conditions, precluding creative thinking – a position ExxonMobil could find itself in. Similarly, a political economy such as Bangladesh can be trapped in its vision of itself and the world, in ways that preclude change on this more systemic level. To change or break out of a particular mindset requires a well-functioning moral imagination on the individual, organizational, and systems levels.

But how do we do all of that while at the same time taking into account situational peculiarities, social context, and the system in which we are embedded? How do we act in a morally reasonable manner and trigger moral imagination? More importantly for this chapter, how does moral imagination work on the organizational and systemic levels?

A good example of this process in practice is the work of Eskom, the South African electric power company. This company was a government-owned all-white-managed company that thrived during apartheid in South Africa, while providing little power service to the non-white community or the rural homeland areas. It did nothing illegal, and indeed, upheld the apartheid laws of South Africa, which, along with its view of profitability, became its boundary conditions. Yet even before the end of apartheid, the company began to evaluate itself and its practices. It was privatized and at the same time became aware of itself as an all-white company with a narrow view of what its service commitments were to a country made up of a largely non-white population. That is, it stepped back from its traditions and practices, it reevaluated itself and its mission, and out of its past practices it began to revise its mental model of what it *should be* as a national power company in a country where the majority of the population was non-white and poor. Eskom began training non-whites for supervisory positions (an activity that was against the law at that time), it experimented with various ways to begin providing electricity throughout the whole country, and it explored ways to make power economically available to the rural poor and to those who had no conception of the value of electricity. Notice again, this is not a completely disinterested perspective. Eskom started with what it knew, electricity, and working within the tradition of apartheid, worked itself out of that perspective. Despite a number of setbacks, Eskom's goals are to electrify all of South Africa, and then to move north to Namibia. As a result, Eskom today is the fifth largest electric utility in the world; it has continued to be economically successful so that it can further experiment with ways to provide service to rural South African communities and develop the expansion of power in other even poorer African nations as well. It is difficult, at best, to pinpoint every individual involved in initiating this change. But one can surely conclude that Eskom changed its mindsets and used a great deal of moral imagination in pushing forward.[23]

Moral imagination, then, is not merely a function of the individual imagination. Rather, moral imagination operates on organizational and systemic levels as well, again as a facilitative mechanism that may encourage sounder moral thinking and moral judgment. It is these latter phases that we have neglected in the first definition of moral imagination. In theoretical terms, moral imagination involves a systemic multiple-perspective approach. This includes the following:

- Concentration on the network of relationships and patterns of interaction, rather than on individual components of particular relationships. Spelling out the networks of relationships from different perspectives.
- A multi-perspective analysis.
- Understanding the various perspectives of the manager, the citizen, the firm, community, state, law, tradition, background institutions, history, and other networks of relationships.
- Taking an evaluative perspective, asking what values are at stake? Which take priority, or should take priority?
- Becoming pro-active both within the system and in initiating structural change.

In this process one should describe the system and its networks of interrelationships to grasp the interconnected nature of the system. One should investigate what is not included in the system (its boundaries and boundary-creating activities) and what mindsets are predominant, asking who are the stakeholders (individuals, associations, organizations, networks, agencies) and what are the core values of each set of stakeholders. Additionally, one needs to outline the core values of the system and speculate as to what these *should* be. Finally, one should think about whether and which organizations or individuals within the system might be capable and willing to risk challenging bits of the system and carrying out change. Thus, moral imagination and systems thinking encourage networked systems analyses that are engaged and critical, creative and evaluative, and values-grounded. It also encourages constructive change within a network of relationships.

There is one more consideration, that of individual responsibility, the responsibilities of the politicians, professionals, managers, and individual citizens. A systems approach should not be confused with some form of abdication of individual responsibility. As individuals, we are not merely the sum of, or identified with, these relationships and roles; we can evaluate and change our relationships, roles, and role obligations, and we are thus responsible for them. That is, each of us is at once a byproduct of, a character in, and an author of, our own experiences. So each of us can examine, evaluate, critique, and find means to change organizations and systems in which we find ourselves.

All of this sounds much too idealistic and impossible, in fact, to achieve. But Muhammad Yunus was able to do exactly that – to change a way of thinking about lending practices to the poor and, as a result, to set up a model for micro lending to the poor that is being emulated in a number of countries.

▲ EXXONMOBIL AND A SYSTEMS APPROACH ▲ TO MORAL IMAGINATION

Let us return to the case with which we began the chapter: ExxonMobil's project in Chad and Cameroon. Given the character of Chad and Cameroon, overridden with poverty, corruption, environmental challenges, fragile indigenous cultures, and the past checkered history of oil exploration in less developed regions, ExxonMobil made the decision to experiment with a new, more systemic approach to this oil exploration project. Deviating from a standard linear stakeholder approach (Figure 7.1), ExxonMobil has created an innovate approach for oil exploration, based on thinking about stakeholder relationships and the corresponding rights and obligations in terms of a complex network of interrelationships (Figure 7.2).

How has ExxonMobil worked on behalf of these interests in the development of the pipeline? ExxonMobil has formed a set of partnerships with the Chad and Cameroon governments, the World Bank, and a number of NGOs. The World Bank's interest is in improving the well-being of the people in Chad and Cameroon. The rationale for considering and then approving the project was that, according to the World Bank:

> [t]his project could transform the economy of Chad ... By 2004, the pipeline would increase Government revenues by 45–50% per year and allow it to use those resources for important investments in health, education, environment, infrastructure, and rural development, necessary to reduce poverty.[24]

The World Bank has set up a series of provisos to ensure that there is sound fiscal management of the revenues received by Chad and Cameroon; it has set up strict environmental and social policies, and has consulted with a number of NGOs involved in the project.

According to a World Bank report, by the middle of 2002 the project employed over 11,000 workers, of whom at least 85 percent are from Chad or Cameroon. Of these local workers, over 3,700 have received high-skills training in construction, electrical, and mechanical trades, and 5 percent of the local workers have supervisory positions. In addition, local businesses have also benefited from the project to a total of almost $100 million. Through the bank, micro lending projects have been developed, accompanied with fiscal and technical training. The aim is to establish permanent micro lending banks.[25] The World Bank, in partnership with ExxonMobil, has created new schools and health clinics, provided vaccines against tuberculosis and medical staff to monitor the distribution, distributed thousands of mosquito nets for protection against malaria, and provided farm implements and seeds to develop indigenous agriculture.[26]

The NGOs involved have goals to improve the economy of Chad and Cameroon, as well as the aim to protect indigenous traditions and the environment. Before approving this venture, the World Bank conducted an extensive series of environmental studies to determine if this project could be done without drastic environmental degradation. It was concluded that with careful drilling and care of the surrounding landscape, and with safety measures that would prevent illicit tapping into the pipeline, the project was environmentally safe. The Chad and Cameroon governments, in turn, pledged to use the profits they received from the venture to improve the standard of living of their citizens. ExxonMobil has hired a former Prime Minister of Chad to coordinate the project, as well as an anthropologist, Ellen Brown, who was in Chad with the Peace Corps some years ago. Under her and other NGO supervision ExxonMobil is building schools, funding clinics, digging wells, fielding AIDS education units, and providing anti-malarial mosquito nets. In some areas where sacred trees are in the way, villagers must give permission to remove the trees and Brown orchestrates chicken sacrifices to preserve the spirit of the trees. (Brown is referred to as Madam Sacrifice by the Chadians.)[27]

Since the partnerships ExxonMobil and the World Bank have created are interdependent, it might be propitious to think of this project as an alliance, an alliance of various players all of whom have important stakes in the project and its outcomes (Figure 7.3).

Figure 7.3 A Stakeholder Alliance Model. Courtesy of Mary Ann Leeper, COO, Female Health Company.

The Perspective of the Critics

The project is not without its problems and critics. According to the Cameroon Environmental Defense (CED) report, there are a number of almost insurmountable negative aspects of this project. Despite good intentions, environmental hazards are inescapable. In any oil-drilling project, even with the strictest safety measures, there will be oil spills. According to World Bank estimates, annual spill rates will be between 1 and 4 percent.[28] There will be increased greenhouse gas emissions, although the level of these has not been accurately calculated. There will also be forestry and bush product losses (e.g., nuts, herbs, and fruit) all of which are to be compensated. In addition, large projects such as these usually spawn an increase in HIV infections and other health risks. Agricultural and livestock losses for displaced farms will occur, although ExxonMobil has guaranteed compensation and/or relocation.

As ExxonMobil, the World Bank, and NGOs working in the region are well aware, there exists no sound rule of law in either country, so that any contracts or promises are not backed with a well-developed legal system to enforce those agreements. This is not only problematic in terms of agreements between the drillers and the government, but there is no legal guarantee that monies given to these governments will actually be spent on citizens' welfare. Indeed, despite World Bank protests, the President of Chad bought arms with his first payment of oil revenue. (He has promised not to do this in the future, but there is no legal framework by which to hold him accountable.)[29]

The CED questions whether adequate compensation is being provided for land use and displacement of people. There have been some intertribal wars between Pygmies and Bantus concerning whose land is actually being compensated. This sort of quarrel upsets the delicate balance between these tribes, and again, there are no enforcement mechanisms to remedy any injustices or thefts. So there are questions concerning the protection of rights and cultural values of indigenous peoples in this region. Even *Fortune* reports that not every citizen will be satisfied with the company's efforts. Even as they begin drilling, local people are complaining that they are not getting jobs, and worries about Pygmy people's (the Baka and Bakola tribes) rights abound.[30]

Both the CED and the Rainforest Action Network question the environmental viability of the project, arguing that issues of water pollution and rain forest protection have not been adequately addressed so that part of the ecosystem may be negatively impacted. Many of the local tribes depend on the forest for food, and changing this ecostructure may not be propitious in preserving these traditional food supplies.[31]

The Required Last Step

It is obvious that the Chad/Cameroon project has moral risks, risks of failure to deliver the benefits to these poor countries, the risk of oil pipe sabotage, and the risk of doing irreparable damage to the environment, despite World Bank studies to the contrary. This set of risks cannot be eliminated, but it can be reduced. When a company undertakes a stakeholder network analysis, it tends to put itself at the center and look at the situation from its point of view,

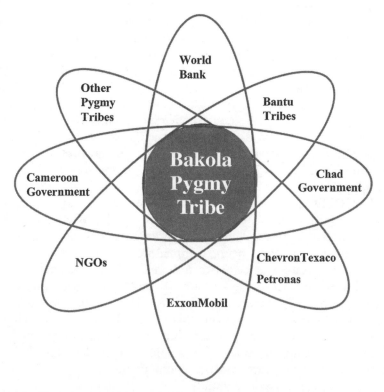

Figure 7.4 Another Stakeholder Alliance Model. Courtesy of Mary Ann Leeper, COO, Female Health Company.

from its mental model as to how the various stakeholders will be affected and how their interests should be balanced. To mitigate the dangers of a biased point of view, one might try to see the world from the perspective of one of the other affected stakeholders as if they were conducting the stakeholder analysis. For example, what decisions would be made if the Bakola Pygmy tribe were doing the stakeholder analysis and that tribe was asking how to balance the interests of its other stakeholders with the interests of ExxonMobil? Quite possibly a different set of decisions would result (see Figures 7.4 and 7.5).

Of course, even this step will not eliminate moral risk. Exxon Mobil still faces the possibility of creating more harm than good in these two countries. Because it is dealing with multiple stakeholders, some of whom are not perfectly honest, in a situation where there are no enforceable legal mechanisms, the company and the World Bank cannot control or mitigate all these risks, although, of course, ExxonMobil will profit extensively from this very rich oil source, and expand the oil supply for its consumers. We would classify this as moral risk since it is hard to calculate, in advance, whether the good of producing oil will balance the harms, and indeed, that may

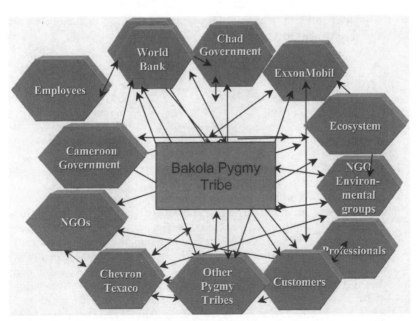

Figure 7.5 Another Network Model.

never be determined with certainty. However, if all these steps were followed ExxonMobil would have attempted to apply a morally imaginative systems approach with some success.

▲ CONCLUSION ▲

To conclude, moral imagination coupled with systems thinking is essential if we are to understand, evaluate, and institute structural, organizational, and individual change. The importance of systems thinking and systems analysis, and this is the final point of the chapter, is to remind ourselves that no organization, system, or subsystem is or need be thought of as a closed static system. Systems thinking is necessary when one tries to apply the stakeholder approach to management ethics, as was recommended in chapter 2. While no such analysis can be complete, nor can we completely escape the historically and culturally constructed mental models in which we operate, this is not a hopeless enterprise. Organizations, institutions, and political economies are dynamic and revisable phenomena, created and changed by individuals. But until we comprehend the complexity of the systemic interrelationships we cannot successfully evaluate the issues in question and begin to make changes that are critical if we are to make moral progress.

▲ NOTES ▲

1. Part of this chapter was originally printed in the *Journal of Business Ethics* in an article entitled, "Moral Imagination and Systems Thinking." It is reproduced with permission of the *Journal*.
2. Transparency International (www.transparency.org). In 2002 they did not list Chad at all!
3. Shell has drilled for oil in Nigeria since 1937, and until recently was the largest oil operation in that country. In the early 1990s its joint venture with Elf and Agip produced over 900,000 barrels of oil a day, most from a region inhabited primarily by the ethnic group, the Ogoni. At the same time, between 1982 and 1992 approximately 1.6 million gallons of oil were spilled in the Nigerian oil fields, some precipitated by dissident Ogoni unhappy with the oil ventures, the environmental degradation, and the lack of improved social impact the drilling had on the local villages and communities. Although Shell claimed to have invested over $100 million on environmental projects in Nigeria, there is little to show

for this investment. Even the *Wall Street Journal* described Ogoniland as "a ravaged environment." (G. Brooks, "Slick Alliance: Shell's Nigerian Fields Produce Few Benefits for Region's Villagers." *Wall Street Journal* [May 6, 1994] reprinted in W. E. Newberry and T. Gladwin, "Shell and Nigerian Oil," in *Ethical Issues in Business*, 7th edition, ed. T. Donaldson, P. Werhane, and M. Cording [Upper Saddle River, NJ: Prentice Hall, 2002], p. 526). Finally, when Shell did not try to intervene or protest the government's assassination of a number of prominent dissidents including Ken Saro-Wiwa, worldwide media attacked Shell for what was perceived to be complicity in these deaths. (Newberry and Gladwin, "Shell and Nigerian Oil," pp. 522–40). Despite $300 billion earned from oil since 1975, Nigeria's per capita income has dropped 23 percent in that time. In 1993, Shell shut down its operations in Ogoniland, but it still drills for oil and gas in other parts of Nigeria. Shell has dramatically revised its code of ethics, it has invested at least $100 million in cleaning up Ogoniland, and has pledged over a half billion dollars in exploring alternate energy sources. (Newberry and Gladwin, "Shell and Nigerian Oil," pp. 535–9).

4. Daniel Fisher, "ExxonMobil's Kazakhstan Quagmire," *Forbes* (online), < www.forbes.com/2003/04/23/cz_df_0423xom.httml >.
5. The Exxon/Mobil case is excerpted from J. Mead, P. Werhane, and A. Wicks, "ExxonMobil in Chad and Cameroon." Darden School Case Bibliography UVA E-2022, 2003.
6. Immanuel Kant, *Critique of Pure Reason*, trans. Norman Kemp Smith (Boston: Bedford/St. Martin's, 1965).
7. Peter Railton, "Moral Realism," *Philosophical Review* 95 (1986), p. 172.
8. Peter Senge, *The Fifth Discipline* (New York: Doubleday, 1990), chapter 10; Deere Gentner and Eric W. Whitley, "Mental Models of Population Growth," in *Environment, Ethics, and Behavior*, ed. Max H. Bazeman, David M. Messick, Ann E. Tenbrunsel, and Kimberley A. Wade-Benzoni (San Francisco: New Lexington Press, 1997), pp. 210–11; Michael Gorman, *Simulating Science* (Bloomington: Indiana University Press, 1992); Mark Johnson, *Moral Imagination* (Chicago: University of Chicago Press, 1993); Patricia H. Werhane, *Moral Imagination and Management Decision-Making* (New York: Oxford University Press, 1999).
9. Karl Weick, *Sensemaking in Organizations* (Thousand Oaks, CA: Sage, 1995); Werhane, *Moral Imagination*.
10. Johnson, *Moral Imagination*, p. 153.
11. Ibid.
12. Werhane, *Moral Imagination*, p. 93.
13. Ibid.
14. David Bornstein, *The Price of a Dream* (Chicago: University of Chicago Press, 1994; 1997).
15. Simon Ramos, *Cure for Chaos* (New York: D. Mackay, 1969), pp. 11–12.

16. Ian I. Mitroff and Harold Linstone, *The Unbounded Mind* (New York: Oxford University Press, 1993).
17. Ibid., chapter 6.
18. Ibid., p. 193.
19. See R. Edward Freeman, "Stakeholder Theory and the Modern Corporation," reprinted in *Ethical Issues in Business*, 6th edition, ed. T. Donaldson and P. H. Werhane (Upper Saddle River, NJ: Prentice-Hall, 1999), pp. 247–57, and Patricia H. Werhane, "Stakeholder Theory and the Ethics of Healthcare Organizations," in *Blackwell's Guide to Business Ethics*, ed. Norman Bowie (Malden, MA: Blackwell, 2001).
20. Patricia H. Werhane, *Persons, Rights, and Corporations* (Englewood Cliffs, NJ: Prentice-Hall, 1985); Peter French, "The Corporation as a Moral Person," *American Philosophical Quarterly* 16 (1979), pp. 207–15.
21. Linda Emanuel, "Ethics and the Structures of Health Care," *Cambridge Quarterly* 9 (2000), pp. 151–68.
22. Senge, *The Fifth Discipline*.
23. Brian Cunningham, "Eskom," Darden School Case Bibliography, 1999. DSCB UVA E 0162, 163, 164, 165, 166.
24. World Bank, 2002. < www.worldbank.org/afr/ccproj/project/ pro_overview.htm > .
25. Ibid.
26. Ibid.; Jerry Useem, "Exxon's African Adventure," *Fortune* (April 15, 2002), pp. 102–14.
27. Ibid., p. 114.
28. AFTE1 Environmental Group. "Project Appraisal Document on a Proposed Credit in the Amount of SDR 4.3 million to the Republic of Cameroon for a Petroleum Environment Enhancement Project." Report no. 19627-CM. World Bank publication, 2000, p. 74.
29. Useem, "Exxon's African Adventure," p. 114.
30. Cameroon Environmental Defense, USA, 2002. "The Chad-Cameroon Oil and Pipeline Project: A Call for Accountability." Publication of the Association Tchadienen pour la Promotion et la Défense des Droits de l'Homme, Chad, Centre pour l'Environnement et le Développement, and Cameroon Environmental Defense, USA.
31. Ibid.; Rainforest Action Network, 2002. < www.ran.org/oilreport/ africa.html > .

chapter eight

Leadership

In this final chapter it is time to put it all together. Many believe that the most important obligation of the manager and the most difficult to achieve is the exercise of leadership. The field of leadership studies is a relatively new field and there is no consensus on the characteristics that make one a leader or on how to teach people to become leaders. Indeed, many would argue that leadership cannot be taught. This position echoes back to Plato, who argued that virtue could not be taught. As evidence for his position, Plato noted that virtuous parents were often unable to raise virtuous sons. In this final chapter, we will endorse a theory of leadership that is consistent with the overall theory of management ethics presented in this book. Before undertaking this task, however, we will review some of the prominent theories of leadership and indicate why we have not endorsed any of them as the theory that is most consistent with the theory of management ethics espoused here.

Must a leader be ethical? Was Hitler a leader? Some, such as Joanne Ciulla, have argued that this question is *the* question of leadership studies.[1] One recalls Machiavelli's advice to the Prince that if one must choose, it is better to be feared than loved. Machiavelli also pointed to many leaders who had been successful in the Italy of the fifteenth century, but had achieved success in highly unethical ways. One even had the uncle who raised him murdered in order achieve his political ambitions. Machiavelli also believed that sometimes the leader had to lie in order to achieve success. For Machiavelli, leadership was the art of staying in power.

Fortunately, we do not need to decide the issue as to whether or not being ethical is part of the definition of leadership. We do not need to decide if Hitler was a leader. What we know is that if Hitler was a leader, he was an unethical one. Since we are seeking ethical managers, we know that leaders should generally not use unethical means to achieve their ends. (We say "generally" because some might argue that leaders sometimes need to behave unethically for the good of those they lead. This dilemma is called the "dirty hands" problem, which we encountered in chapter 1.) And ethical leadership is certainly not a matter of simply staying in power. In fact we will argue that ethical leadership has little to do with power as it is conventionally understood.

Some would claim that the leader should be a visionary and ideally a charismatic visionary. The ethical manager need not be either a visionary or charismatic and there are real moral dangers if he or she is. First, the ethical manager needs an ethical vision and not just any vision. If a leader has an unethical vision, being charismatic in getting followers to endorse that vision only makes matters worse. Charisma is defined as "a rare personal quality of leaders who arouse fervent popular devotion and enthusiasm." It is also defined as "personal magnetism or charm." Unfortunately, one of the more charismatic leaders in human history was Hitler. Ethical leadership is not about being charismatic and it is not a matter of being a visionary. If one is charismatic and has a vision, one ought to have a vision that stands up under ethical scrutiny.

This point has some real bite. In his recent book, *Good to Great*, Jim Collins and his research team identified 11 companies that had performed three times better than the market over a period of 15 years. These were the only companies he could find that met these criteria. One of these companies is Philip Morris – a company that is great at selling what Collins calls "sinful" products – tobacco, beer, chocolate, and coffee. The leaders of Philip Morris had decided to be great at selling "sinful" products (that was their vision in my terms) and they were passionate about it. As Collins reports, "In 1979 Ross Millhiser, then vice chairman of Philip Morris and a dedicated smoker, said, 'I love cigarettes. It's one of the things that makes life worth living.'" A vision of greatness pursued with passion (recognizing that passion is weaker than charisma) has led to success that places Philip Morris among the great companies in financial terms. But are the CEOs of Philip Morris ethical managers? Many would say not.

One need not criticize charismatic visionary leadership by criticizing the product produced. Champions of human autonomy would argue that none of these "sinful" products is illegal and that consumers are free to choose whether to buy them or not. The revelations of deception and marketing to minors that have plagued the tobacco companies in recent years call into question that argument. But let us accept the value of human autonomy as a goal that ethical leaders should support. The reader may recall that we developed a theory of autonomy with respect to Kant's moral philosophy in chapter 3. At that point we argued that autonomy was the basis of Kantian ethics. Our characterization of autonomy in chapter 3 also applies here. In this chapter we will focus on the fact that the fully autonomous person has access to the facts and makes decisions on the basis of reasoning. Charismatic leadership does not motivate by providing access to facts for rational evaluation; it motivates by emotional enthusiasm. For those who take the exercise of freedom as an ultimate human value, as both Nobel Prize-winners Milton Friedman and Amartya Sen do, charismatic leadership could not be the ethical ideal. The ethical ideal is leadership that respects and promotes the autonomy of its followers.

James Macgregor Burns is undoubtedly the dean of leadership studies. In his writings he distinguishes transactional leadership from transformational leadership. Transactional leadership occurs when the leader sees possibilities for exchange and thus approaches followers with an eye to exchanging one thing for another. The exchange could be jobs for votes or subsidies for campaign contributions. Burns notes that these exchanges can be economic, political, or psychological in nature. Under this view the leader is a successful manager of a mutually beneficial transaction.

Transformational leadership is very different. At one point Burns defines transformational leadership as a "relationship of mutual stimulation and elevation that converts followers into leaders and may convert leaders into moral agents."[2] Thus, under transformational leadership, both the leader and the follower are presumably changed for the better. Burns has been influenced by Lawrence Kohlberg and the moral development school. Kohlberg was a moral psychologist who believed that people could evolve through higher stages of morality, although relatively few reached the highest stage – that of principled moral reasoning. One of the goals of transformational leadership is to tap into values that are higher than the ones the followers – and quite possibly the leader – are operating on. At the highest level, appeals are made to such deeply held values as justice, liberty, and brotherhood.

What separates Burns from many in the leadership area is how he would motivate followers to the higher levels of morality. It would not be done out of fear (Machiavelli), from indoctrination, or from charisma; it would involve the leader's interaction with followers and an appeal to higher values. Getting everyone on board would occur through participation – one of the principles of moral management endorsed in chapter 3.

There is much to accept in Burns's theory of transformational leadership. Morality is central to the concept. His rejection of indoctrination shows that he respects the autonomy of the followers – another principle of moral management. To some extent, the followers participate as all strive to a higher vision. However, a number of issues are not sufficiently addressed. Who decides what counts as higher values? Kohlberg has been criticized for giving traditionally masculine values the highest place in moral development. Some research has shown that women ranked consistently lower in moral development. However, Carol Gilligan, among others, has argued that the lower score does not result from the fact that women are less morally developed than men. Indeed, there is evidence that the opposite is true. Gilligan argues that women are more committed to relationships and thus have an ethics of caring. They make decisions that are based more on preserving the relationship than they are on principles. One could interpret Burns as saying that the leader has, or at least sees, a higher set of values and then transforms the followers so that they too adopt these higher values. For Burns, the content of the values may be more important than the process for getting there.

Suppose a minority of followers does not accept the higher values. What should the leader do then? It seems that the minority must somehow be brought around. It seems that the other alternative for Burns is to remove the minority from the organization. There does not seem to be a large place for disagreement and dissent between leaders and followers. We would prefer a theory of leadership that allows a place for disagreement and dissent.

All the leadership theories considered thus far maintain the hierarchical division between leaders and followers. As we saw in chapter 3, there is always a danger that those higher up in the hierarchy will use those lower down for their own ends. In the terms of the philosophy of Immanuel Kant, there is always a danger that the leader will use the follower as merely a means to the follower's end. Perhaps the CEO's goal is to be a great company by producing the best product of that kind. Ethical leadership is more than greatness in that sense. The ethical leaders achieve their ends without treating the various stakeholders as mere means to the end or vision.

Perhaps ethical leadership involves an inversion of the traditional hierarchy between leader and follower. Perhaps the ethical leader should be the servant rather than the leader. The theorist Robert Greenleaf has espoused such a theory of servant leadership. Greenleaf points out that the idea for servant leadership came from his reading of Herman Hesse's *Journey to the East*. In that book the central figure Leo turns out to be a leader because, although he does menial chores, only Leo can make it possible for the group to conclude its journey. Greenleaf puts the main point this way:

> But to me, this story clearly says that the great leader is seen as a servant first, and that simple fact is the key to his greatness. Leo was actually the leader all of the time, but he was servant first because that was what he was deep down inside. Leadership was bestowed upon a man who was by nature a servant.

Although contrary to the "great man" theories of leadership, this view of leadership does have its adherents. Max DePree, Peter Senge, Margaret Wheatley, Warren Bennis, and Frances Hesselbein have all endorsed the concept.

But servant leadership is not without ethical dangers. If it is wrong to use another merely to achieve your own ends, it is equally wrong to allow yourself to be used merely as the means to achieve the ends of another. In either case, a person is being used as a means merely and that is morally wrong. The danger of the servant leader is that he or she would allow him- or herself to be used as a means merely. There is a danger that in being a servant one becomes servile and Kant specifically rejects servility as a moral position. Kant says:

> A low opinion of oneself in relation to others is no humility; it is a sign of little spirit and of a servile character. To flatter oneself that this is a virtue is to mistake an imitation for the genuine article; it is a monk's virtue and not at all natural; this form of humility is in fact a form of pride. There is nothing unjust or unreasonable in self-esteem.[3]

Now we do not think the danger of servant leadership is that CEOs or even middle managers will become servile; the greater danger is that they will become a servant to the organization in a slavish way. An example of this phenomenon is the workaholic CEO who totally sacrifices the lives of his family and indeed his own life for the good of the business. If servant leadership involves that kind of sacrifice it is not ethical. Ethical leadership is leadership that reflects what we now call a good work/life balance. One of the great corporate leaders who recognizes this fact is the former CEO of Medtronic, Bill George.[4]

Recently Jim Collins, in his book *Good to Great*, has endorsed a leadership style that bears some analogies to servant leadership, although he would never use that term. In his study of the 11 great companies, Collins was surprised to discover that "larger-than-life, celebrity leaders who ride in from the outside are *negatively* correlated with taking a company from good to great."[5] He also noticed that the CEOs who had made their companies great were people hardly anyone had heard of. How many names do you recognize from this list: George Cain, Alan Wurtzel, David Maxwell, Colman Mockler, Darwin Smith, Jim Herring, Lyle Everingham, Joe Cullman, Fred Allen, Cork Walgreen, and Carl Reichardt?[6]

All of these CEOs exemplified what Collins refers to as step 5 leadership. The lower four steps in the leadership pyramid, starting with the base, are (1) capable individual, (2) contributing team member, (3) competent manager, and (4) effective leader. One of the defining characteristics of step 5 leadership is humility:

> Level 5 leaders channel their ego needs away from themselves and into the larger goal of building a great company. It's not that level 5 leaders have no ego or self-interest. Indeed, they are incredibly ambitious – but their ambition is first and foremost for the institution, not themselves.[7]

Collins noted that step 5 leaders almost never talked about themselves, and behaved in ways very different from the more typical leaders. They take no credit when things go well but take complete responsibility when things go badly. Collins refers to this as the phenomenon of the window and the mirror. Step 5 leaders look out the window to find who deserves credit but they look in the mirror to discover who deserves blame.

Another feature of step 5 leadership is that these leaders set up their successors for success rather than failure. Finally, step 5 leaders have an iron will.

This humility that does not equal servility is a desirable trait for ethical leadership. Step 5 leaders would not put their own interests ahead of their obligations to other corporate stakeholders. They would not violate the obligations that go with the role of being a manager. Those executives we discussed in chapter 1, who enriched themselves at the expense of employees and/or shareholders, were not humble people. Wealth and fame were needed to feed their egos.

But being a humble leader with an iron will is not sufficient for being an ethical leader. Although Collins points out that the step 5 leader gets the right people on board and enforces discipline without being dictatorial, the step 5 leader is not necessarily concerned with the morality of the company's product or with the autonomy of employees. One of the great companies is Philip Morris – a major producer of tobacco products. And most of Collins's great companies are hierarchical. Such observations confirm our insistence that sustained financial success is not sufficient for ethical management. Financial success must be achieved in an appropriate way. Having said this, one measure of a leader's success is his or her ability. A moral leader cannot ignore the bottom line or the obligations that corporate leaders have to stockholders.

Another variation of the theory of servant leadership is to view the leader as a teacher or educator. This view is held by James O'Toole and is naturally attractive to those of us in academic positions. Before endorsing such view we would need to know which of the many theories of teaching or educating would be endorsed. As Lisa Newton has pointed out,[8] education can take place in at least two ways. Some teachers try to impose the correct beliefs and values on students. Others are more process-oriented and believe that education is primarily about getting students to think for themselves. Since we hold that individual autonomy is an intrinsic value and argue below that the ideal of ethical managerial leadership is to enhance autonomy, the indoctrination model of education is not acceptable.

On the other hand, there is much to be said in favor of the moral acceptability of a theory of leadership that is built on the analogy of the Socratic educator. In learning to think for oneself, one is exercising one's autonomy, and by expanding the range of options one is actually enhancing individual autonomy. There is another benefit of getting students to think for themselves. Independent thinking is important in developing a sense of personal responsibility. Traditionally, a major justification for liberal arts education has been that it prepares leaders, especially leaders who have a sense of civic responsibility and will be leaders in the wider community. Thus, this view of leadership fits in well with our earlier arguments, that managers do have an obligation to be socially responsible.

However, independent thinking can go astray. Ethical managerial leadership needs to be more than process. Content, the thoughts of independent thinkers, needs to be considered as well. Also the teacher/student model is usually a hierarchical one with the teacher as an authority figure. Thus, the leader as teacher or educator is not quite up to the task of providing a full-blown theory of ethical managerial leadership.

Neither leadership that perpetuates a hierarchy nor leadership that inverts the hierarchy between leader and follower represents the ideal of ethical leadership. The ideal of ethical leadership is one that supports basic ethical values within the business organization. Since freedom or autonomy represents a basic value in economics, political philosophy, and ethics, let us take freedom as a basic value to be realized within business – a position that characterizes this entire book. As we saw in chapter 3 and elsewhere, the philosopher who builds his or her ethical theory on the presupposition of human freedom and its intrinsic value is Immanuel Kant. What would ethical leadership look like if it were consistent with Kant's moral philosophy?

We believe that Kant's third formulation of the categorical imperative – the formulation that Kant believed encompassed the first two formulations – will provide the theory of ethical leadership we need. The third formulation – often referred to as the kingdom of ends formulation – asserts that "one should act as if one were a member of an ideal kingdom of ends in which one was subject and sovereign at the same time." Kant recognized that human beings (means) interacted with other human beings (ends). The arena of interaction is the kingdom of ends. In a business organization the interaction is among persons, the same as it is in any other organization. Since people are moral creatures deserving of respect and dignity, they cannot be treated simply as economic entities. They cannot be simply used as the means to economic ends.

But how do we respect one another in an organization that is viewed as an ideal kingdom of ends. The rules for making the decisions as to how the organization is to be managed need to be ones that can be publicly advocated and endorsed by all those in the organization. In that sense each person in the organization is a sovereign because he or she endorsed the process for making the rules that will govern the organization. And each person is subject because he or she is subject to those rules that have been endorsed by him or her and others. What this means is that the rules governing the organization cannot simply be imposed on the basis of power or superiority of position. The rules must be the kind of norms that could in principle receive the consent of all rational moral beings and thus be acceptable to all. This kingdom of ends formulation of the categorical imperative acts as a significant restraint on leadership as it is traditionally understood. It means the leader should be a decision proposer rather than a decision imposer. The leader needs to get buy-in, but that buy-in should come voluntarily and not be imposed on the basis of authority of position or power.

Before developing this idea further and applying it to a theory of leadership, some points of clarification are needed in order to avoid misunderstanding. We are arguing that ethical leadership involves a form of participative management and the ethical leader creates the conditions for participative management.

But is participative management not the abandonment of leadership? And even if it were not, would not such leadership lead to chaos? If you need universal buy-in for every decision that is made in the organization, you have anarchy and the organization will fail. That is certainly true, but universal buy-in is not required for every decision. We need to distinguish among the following:

1. The individual decision, e.g., how many motors should we order?
2. The norm for making a decision, e.g., should that decision be left to the purchasing department?
3. How should the norms in (2) be made?

At a minimum there should be participative management with respect to (3) and often with respect to (2). By placing the emphasis on (3) we give due respect to differences in skills and ability. The sales manager does need a say in whether a certain product meets the company's quality standards. That determination takes expertise that is not available to everyone in the organization. But all members of the organization can and should have a say in the governing rule that turns certain decisions over to experts. However, it is important to note that participative management is not equivalent to democratic decision-making for all decisions in the organization.

Moreover, as an ideal the Kantian leader should push decision-making down the organization chart so that everyone can be a leader.

Under quality circles and open-book management, as well as in much Japanese management, some decisions are best made on the assembly line itself, including who to hire for the team.

The following principles are ones that should be acceptable to all rational moral beings and may constitute principles of type (3) above:

1. The leader should consider the interest of all the affected stakeholders in any decision he or she makes.
2. The leader should have those affected by the firm's rules and policies participate in the determination of those rules and policies before they are implemented, and upon being implemented they should be periodically reviewed by representatives of the various stakeholder groups.
3. It should not be the case that the leader always gives the interests of one stakeholder group priority.
4. When a situation arises where it appears that the interest of one set of stakeholders must be sacrificed for the interests of others, the leader cannot make that decision solely on the basis that there is a greater number of people in one stakeholder group than in another.
5. Every leader must in cooperation with others in the organization establish procedures to ensure that relations among the stakeholders are governed by the rules of justice.[9]

The first principle is a straightforward requirement that leaders take respect for persons seriously. That principle says that leaders should take the moral point of view. The second principle provides a practical way for the leader to respect the autonomy of followers. The third principle functions as a principle of legitimacy since it insures that all those involved in the firm receive some minimum benefit from being part of the organization. The principle also reminds us that the leader is not to use participants to achieve the greater good when those participants receive no benefit from the public good. The fourth principle is even more clearly anti-utilitarian. Principle 5 ensures that where there is disagreement about the laws or norms that should govern the organization, the disagreements should be settled on grounds of justice. This principle acts as a further check on an authoritarian leader.

These principles are negative principles of constraint. They act as a check on an authoritarian leader. But they can also be used to provide a positive theory of ethical leadership. The ethical leader should respect the autonomy of his or her followers. If one is to do that to the fullest extent, what would ethical leadership look like? We contend that the moral ideal is for the leader to aim at driving leadership down the organizational chart. The ethical ideal is for the leader to turn followers into leaders. The conventional view is that one looks to the leader to make decisions. On that view the ethical manager is the one who makes good (ethically defensible) decisions. However, on the view espoused here, the leader turns followers into decision-makers. On this view the ethical manager is the one who enhances the autonomy and self-respect of those who were followers by making them partners in the decision-making process.

One might think that this suggestion is impractical. The last thing one needs in an organization that has to be responsive to ever changing conditions in a highly competitive international environment is diffuse decision-making – or so one might think. Critics of our view of leadership might respond by arguing that decision-making in a corporation should not resemble a faculty meeting. However, there are actual cases in the literature where this view of leadership has been implemented. There is also some empirical evidence in support of the theory.

Studies show that decision-making is improved if there is collaboration and discussion. One study shows that in airline emergencies decision-making is improved if the captain discusses what should be done with the first officer. The results hold so long as there is as little as eight seconds to make a decision. No major business decision needs to be made in eight seconds.

Our first business example is somewhat tainted. Percy Barnevik, the former CEO of Asea Brown Boveri, is one of Europe's most successful CEOs. He exemplifies the leadership strategy we recommend for ideal ethical management. Unfortunately, upon retiring he received an extravagant retirement package that had not been disclosed to the full board. However, that moral lapse does not take away from the ethical nature of his leadership strategy.

Barnevik's leadership style is exhibited in the Harvard Business School case ABB Relays. The case is often used to teach the theory of the matrix organization, but it is equally effective as a case study on leadership. Here is how the case unfolds. Barnevik is the chief protagonist in the case, but by page 2 Barnevik disappears. The case is 12 pages long, excluding appendices. By page 2, the actor at center stage is Göran Lindahl, Asea's executive vice-president. As the case unfolds it is clear the Barnevik has made Lindahl a leader. For example, Lindahl is responsible for communicating the new philosophy and principles, including the guiding principle of decentralization. He also wanted to emphasize the guiding principle of individual accountability. He delegated a series of tasks to managers at lower levels and gave them real responsibility. By page 6, Lindahl disappears and Ulf Gundemark, who becomes ABB's business head for the worldwide relay business, is at the center of the action. Leadership is being pushed down the organization chart. A focal event in the case centers on the allocation of export markets. The Swiss company has been given the responsibility for coordinating sales into Mexico, but a dispute arose concerning the shortening of the company's lines to its customers and minimizing the non-value-added work in the system. Gundemark delegated this to a team of four marketing managers. After much negotiation, they reported back to Gundemark that they could not reach a decision. The conventional response to this situation is for Gundemark to make the decision. After all, is that not what the leader is supposed to do rather than have subordinates waste more time on the matter? But that is not how Gundemark behaved. Rather than make the decision himself, he sent them back for further discussion. Several days later, after exhausting negotiations, they reported they had reached a majority decision of three to one. But Gundemark wanted a decision acceptable to all – in other words, a unanimous decision. Finally, after three more days of intense negotiation, the marketing team came back with a unanimous recommendation. Talk about a decision where you are both subject and sovereign.

Another example is Jan Carlzon, former head of SAS airlines. When Carlzon took over, SAS had lost its way and was floundering. He undertook a number of steps that brought popularity and thus profitability to the airline. A characteristic of his leadership style was to empower others in the organization to make decisions. One story in particular reflects Carlzon's leadership style. Upon taking a hard-earned vacation, he realized that he had not succeeded as the kind of leader he wanted to be. Those people who wanted him to make a decision constantly interrupted his vacation. Carlzon realized that he would succeed only when he went on vacation and no one called to seek his advice. His job as a leader was to encourage subordinates to make decisions on their own. Eventually he went on vacation and no one called. Carlzon's book *Moments of Truth* begins as follows:

Everyone needs to know and feel that he is needed. Everyone wants to be treated as an individual. Giving someone the freedom to take responsibility releases resources that would otherwise remain concealed. An individual without information cannot take responsibility; an individual who is given information cannot help but take responsibility.[10]

Carlzon's insights fit well with the ethical perspective taken by this book. The ethical manager must treat each stakeholder as an individual and treat the autonomy of those individuals with respect. Although we have emphasized giving leadership responsibility to employees, an ideal might be to promote the autonomy of all stakeholder groups. Robert Frederick has suggested this idea. In his version of stakeholder theory, R. Edward Freeman has recommended a board composed of stakeholder representatives. Governance suggestions such as that one fit well with the overall theme of this book.

There are also strategic and organizational reasons to adopt the theory of leadership espoused here. In an autocratic hierarchical structure, criticism and dissent are not tolerated. In that situation there is always a possibility for the phenomenon of groupthink. In groupthink an organization may go down a disastrous path because it does not provide an environment for criticism internally and it sees external criticism as a battle of us against them. Many believe that the Challenger disaster may have been caused at least in part by groupthink. The recent report on the Columbia disaster indicates that not much has changed at NASA since the loss of the Challenger in 1986. Psychological studies have shown that the best preventative for groupthink is an atmosphere that encourages critical evaluation. Kantian leadership is the kind of leadership that best supports this atmosphere of critical evaluation.

The passing of the Sarbanes–Oxley Act has provided yet another pragmatic reason to take the view of leadership espoused in this chapter seriously. In an authoritarian hierarchical organization where there is also disagreement about what a firm ought to do, there is always a danger that the disgruntled employee will engage in an act of whistle-blowing. Whistle-blowing has often been equivalent to sacrificing one's career in the industry, so whistle-blowing has been rather rare and perhaps not a major management concern. With the spate of moral scandals in 2002 and 2003 and the resulting Sarbanes–Oxley Act, all that has changed. Whistle-blowers are given specific protection under the Act. *Time* characterized 2002 as the year of the whistle-blower, and three women whistle-blowers were *Time*'s "man of the year" in 2002.

It is often said that whistle-blowing results from a failure of management. What kind of leadership is most likely to prevent this management failure? A leadership style that encourages critical discussion and then consensus, or in the absence of consensus on a specific issue, consensus on how to reach a decision. In other words, at a minimum, critical discussion and consensus on how decisions are to be made is required. Leadership that encourages participative management and respects the autonomy of individuals – in other words, Kantian-style management is required.

▲ CONCLUSION ▲

We believe that ethical management requires a radical rethinking of management styles. First and foremost, managers must realize that they are not in business to aggrandize wealth at the expense of those for whom they are agents. Management brings with it a set of role-related expectations and obligations. Managers have obligations to all their corporate stakeholders. The key to ethical management is to respect persons and to value their autonomy as voluntary participants in the business enterprise. In the preceding chapters we have tried to indicate – at least in a general way – some of the more specific obligations for managers that result when a respect for persons' philosophy is implemented. As managers become leaders, we have asked what kind of leadership style is most appropriate for ethical management. We have rejected the "great man" theory that idolized the likes of Jack Welch. Instead, a leader in the Kantian tradition would seek to push leadership through the organization by sharing information and by sharing decision-making. That is what the ethical manager does.

▲ NOTES ▲

1. Joanne Ciulla, "Leadership Ethics: Mapping the Territory," in *Ethics: The Heart of Leadership*, ed. Joanne Ciulla (New York: Praeger, 1998).
2. James MacGregor Burns, *Leadership* (New York: Harper and Row, 1978).
3. Immanuel Kant, *Lectures on Ethics,* trans. Louis Infield (New York:

Harper & Row, 1963).

4. See William W. George, *Authentic Leadership: Rediscovering the Secrets to Creating Lasting Value* (San Francisco: Jossey-Bass, 2003).

5. Jim Collins, *Good to Great* (New York: Harper Business, 2001), p. 10.

6. Ibid., p. 28.

7. Ibid., p. 21.

8. Lisa Newton, "Moral Leadership in Business: the Role of Structure," *Business and Professional Ethics Journal* 5 (1985), pp. 74–90.

9. These principles are based on Norman Bowie's principles for a moral firm. See Bowie, *Business Ethics: A Kantian Perspective* (Malden, MA: Blackwell, 1999).

10. Jan Carlzon, *Moments of Truth* (Cambridge, MA: Ballinger, 1987). We recognize that as leadership is pushed down the organization it is important that the CEO not lose his or her ability to have the information required to perform his or her job. Information needs to be pushed down the organization but it needs to be pushed up the organization as well.

Index